Gerbils as a Hobby

by Laurie Holland

SAVE-OUR-PLANET SERIES

T.F.H. Publications, Inc.
1 T.F.H. Plaza • Third & Union Aves. • Neptune, NJ 07753

Contents

Photography: Dr. Herbert R. Axelrod, Bob Bernhard, Michael Gilroy, R. Hanson, Horst Mayer, D.J. Robinson, and Vince Serbin.

Distributed in the UNITED STATES to the Pet Trade by T.F.H. Publications, Inc., One T.F.H. Plaza, Neptune City, NJ 07753; distributed in the UNITED STATES to the Bookstore and Library Trade by National Book Network, Inc. 4720 Boston Way, Lanham MD 20706; in CANADA to the Pet Trade by H & L Pet Supplies Inc., 27 Kingston Crescent, Kitchener, Ontario N2B 2T6; Rolf C. Hagen Ltd., 3225 Sartelon Street, Montreal 382 Quebec; in CANADA to the Book Trade by Macmillan of Canada (A Division of Canada Publishing Corporation), 164 Commander Boulevard, Agincourt, Ontario M1S 3C7; in the United Kingdom by T.F.H. Publications, PO Box 15, Waterlooville PO7 6BQ; in AUSTRALIA AND THE SOUTH PACIFIC by T.F.H. (Australia), Pty. Ltd., Box 149, Brookvale 2100 N.S.W., Australia; in NEW ZEALAND by Brooklands Aquarium Ltd. 5 McGiven Drive, New Plymouth, RD1 New Zealand; in Japan by T.F.H. Publications, Japan—Jiro Tsuda, 10-12-3 Ohjidai, Sakura, Chiba 285, Japan; in SOUTH AFRICA by Multipet Pty. Ltd., P.O. Box 35347, Northway, 4065, South Africa. Published by T.F.H. Publications, Inc.

Manufactured in the United States of America by T.F.H. Publications, Inc.

Pink-eyed white gerbil.

Introduction

The popular little rodent that is known as the gerbil, or the clawed, or mid-day, jird is one of many similar animals that inhabit most semi-desert areas of Africa and Asia. Although the Mongolian gerbil, which is the one most commonly kept as a pet, was first discovered during the 19th century, it was not until comparatively recent times that it was in fact established as a pet. As such, it is the newest of what might be termed the major pets that you can choose from at this time.

As its name would suggest, the Mongolian gerbil is from the country of that name. All present-day pet gerbils are thought to have descended from a small group of them that were captured and sent to Japan for research study. From there, some were exported to the USA and then to the UK and mainland Europe. The gerbil's history is thus not unlike that of its relative, the hamster, in that all pet hamsters seen today are descended from just a few wild-caught specimens.

However, the gerbil, unlike

Meet the gerbil, a delightful little pet whose native habitat is the desert-like regions of Africa and Asia. The Mongolian gerbil, shown here, is one of the best-known species of gerbil.

The virtues of gerbils are numerous. They are sociable animals that get along well together, they are clean, and their overall general care is fairly simple.

the hamster, has the virtue of being a very sociable little creature that will happily live alongside its fellows without fighting them continually. It is also less likely to nip you when you handle it, though in fairness to any rodent, this depends to a large degree on how often such pets are handled, and from what age. At this time the gerbil is not quite as popular as a pet as either mice or hamsters, but the situation is changing as new color mutations appear. They always supply impetus to a given pet species as they increase the number of people who find the new colors appealing.

Gerbils are very easy to care for in terms of their housing and feeding needs. They are also very reliable breeders, very clean in

their personal habits, and extremely inquisitive pets. They are not expensive to purchase, so all in all they have many virtues that are recommendable. Having kept and bred all of the popular rodents, I would not suggest that the gerbil as a pet is either superior or inferior to either mice or hamsters. Rather, it is a matter of its being different.

With its well-furred tail that sports a small brush and its long hind legs, the gerbil is a cute little animal that has no negatives associated with it. At this time the range of colors is not as extensive as in other popular rodents, but there is enough choice to appeal to most enthusiasts—and to provide a good challenge to potential color breeders. Within the following chapters you will find all of the information you are likely to need for keeping and breeding gerbils, whether as pets, or as potential exhibition animals. If the advice given is taken, you will enjoy many years of pleasure derived from your involvement with these enchanting little rodents.

Gerbil Zoology

The gerbil is a member of the zoological order of animals called Rodentia—the rodents. This is by far the most successful order of mammals on our planet, embracing possibly 60% of all mammals in terms of

are very adaptable, both in terms of their environment and in their temperature tolerance. They have a high reproductive rate, and most species of them are extremely cosmopolitan in their eating habits. Many

While it is true that gerbils are rodents, they certainly do not possess the negative qualities associated with other rodents such as rats and mice. For example, they do not spread disease.

the number of species. Most rodents are relatively small creatures, but the capybara of South America, at 1.2m (4 ft.), is an exception to this comment. Rodents are found throughout the world and in just about every ecological niche—from steamy jungles to frozen wastelands.

Their tremendous success as an order stems from a few important evolutionary reasons. They

rodent species have gained from human preeminence on the planet. Apart from their being transported—not always by choice—as humans traveled from one part of the earth to another, humans have also helped many rodents, such as mice and rats, by killing thousands of the rodent's natural enemies.

Wolves, foxes, snakes, polecats, wild cats, and predatory birds that would ordinarily have devoured

These two gerbils demonstrate the alert posture that is typical for them and for other rodents as well.

millions of rodents have been systematically persecuted by us humans, and this has been very much to the advantage of rodents. The fact that we also store vast quantities of foods (such as grain) has likewise given many rodents an excellent source of food as well as a place to reside.

BASIC ANATOMICAL FEATURES

The main feature that separates rodents from most other mammals is their dental arrangement. Rodents have elongated paired incisors in the upper and lower jaws. They have no canine teeth: there is a gap where the canine teeth normally appear in mammals. This space is called a diastema and allows rodents to draw in their cheeks behind the incisors as they gnaw.

Premolars may or may not be present (gerbils have none). The gerbil has three molars on each side of the upper and lower jaws, thus giving it a total (counting the incisors) of sixteen teeth.

The incisor teeth grow throughout the life of the rodent. The enamel on the inner surface of the teeth is soft, so it wears away disproportionately to that on the outer edge. This ensures that the teeth stay razor sharp for gnawing purposes.

Another modification to the anatomy of rodents is in relation to their digestive system, which contains a much-enlarged intestinal pouch called the cecum. This organ contains cellulose-digesting organisms, or flora, which act on the rigid cellular walls of plants in order to make them digestible. The secretions from the cecum mix with foods to soften them. In order to gain maximum benefit from their food, many rodents pass from their bodies special pellets that are eaten and sent around the digestive system a second time. These pellets are not fecal matter, but a novice who sees rodents eat what appears to be feces may not appreciate this fact. The process is known as coprophagy or refection, and is equivalent to rumination seen in ungulates, such as cows, when they chew cud.

Other anatomical features of rodents are similar to most other mammals. Gerbils reproduce in the same manner—they are placental, meaning that the young develop within the female until they reach a quite advanced state. Gerbils have moderately good eye sight, and their hearing and sense of smell are well developed. Being creatures of arid zones, they are adapted to conserve moisture: their urine is concentrated. It is regulated by the amount of moisture within their foods. Gerbils, like cats and other animals evolved in dry regions, are able to reduce the amount of water lost from cells through osmosis and sweating. This reduces their need to drink large quantities, so they are able to stay in what is termed water balance. Dogs, humans, and other animals from regions where water is plentiful lose much water during activity and body metabolism so they must drink copiously in order to stay in balance. However,

Gerbils have keen senses of hearing and smell, and their eyesight is fairly good.

this does not mean that pet gerbils should not have access to water on a 24-hour basis: it should be available at all times.

Gerbils' adaptation to dry environments does mean that they suffer more than

defined groups known as suborders. One of them is called Myomorpha and contains such animals as rats, mice, doormice, jerboas, and both hamsters and gerbils. These many rodents are placed into one

A black gerbil. There are over 80 species of gerbil found in several regions around the world.

"wet region" animals if the air becomes very humid. They are, therefore, more intolerant of excess dampness or a humidity reading in excess of 50% than are dogs, for example. (Dogs are able to shed excess moisture through sweat glands and by panting, neither of which is a feature of gerbils and other similar rodents.)

GERBIL CLASSIFICATION

The order Rodentia is divided into three rather ill-

of nine families in the suborder. The family containing hamsters, gerbils, lemmings, voles, and some rats is called Cricetidae. This family is again divided into numerous subfamilies, the gerbil being in that known as Gerbillinae.

There are probably in excess of 80 species of gerbils, and they are found scattered throughout Europe, Africa, and Asia. The subfamily is divided into numerous groups known as genera (singular, genus). They contain such gerbils as the great gerbils of the genus *Rhombomys*, the naked soled gerbils of the genus *Taterillus*, the Egyptian gerbils of the genus *Gerbillus*, and the gerbils of the genus *Meriones*. The last genus just noted includes the Mongolian gerbil, or mid-day jird, *Meriones unguiculatus*, which is the subject of this book. Among other gerbils in this genus are the Persian jird, *M. persicus*, and Tristram's jird, *M. tristami*.

The more exotic gerbils are, of course, much more expensive to purchase and may require considerably larger accommodations; they are really more suited to the specialist rodent keeper than to the pet owner.

You may wonder why all zoological names of animals and plants are in Latin. This is because this language was used by scholars many years ago when the original system of classifying animals was evolved by Carolus Linnaeus, a Swedish naturalist. It is totally accepted by all nations, thus it is international in application. Whereas common names, such as large, great, naked soled, Egyptian, Indian, or Mongolian, could be applied to numerous different species, scientific names, such as *Meriones unguiculatus*, are very specific to a definite species. Confusion is thus avoided by utilizing a carefully-thought-out system of identification, which the binomial system of classification provides. A species is always identified by the use of two names. One is the genus, the other the specific or trivial name. The two together are unique to a given animal. They are printed

The Mongolian Gerbil, *Meriones unguiculatus*, is a very reasonably priced gerbil that is a good choice for the average pet owner.

in a text that differs from that of the main text, which is why you will see scientific names in italics.

GERBILS IN THE WILD

Mongolian gerbils, like many others in the genus, are gregarious animals and live in family units. These units may comprise a few males, a larger number of females, and a collection of youngsters. Mongolian gerbils live in burrows, which they either dig out themselves or which have been vacated by other small burrowing animals. The gerbils venture out at dawn or dusk when the temperature is not too high. They will search for the seeds of plants, fruits and roots, as well as for any other edible foods such as invertebrates (bugs, worms, and their like) that may be in the vicinity of their territory.

The burrow will normally feature at least two exits and contains areas for sleeping, for food storage,

In the wild, gerbils gather their food at night and spend the daytime in tunnels, where they can escape from the heat.

and a toilet room. The burrows may sometimes be very extensive if a family group has grown in numbers over the years. In order to overcome any problems that might be created by inbreeding, females will occasionally leave the group and mate with males from nearby families and then return to their own families. Other than such occasions, gerbils do not allow other gerbils to join their family units. Once a small colony has grown to large numbers, some of the youngsters will wander farther afield in order to find better feeding grounds. They will then start their own family group. By this process, which is common to many animals, the species slowly extends its range. However, natural barriers such as mountains and rivers limit the outward progression of a range. It is also restricted by competition from other similar species. The numbers of gerbils are kept in check by disease and, of course, by their many predators: snakes, owls and other predatory birds, foxes, cats, and even other rodents, such as rats.

The defense strategy of a gerbil is essentially of three types. It can seek the refuge of its burrow, or of rocks and logs, it can take flight and try to outrun its enemies, or it can make long hops and jumps. When confronted by snakes, it may also use its long rear legs to kick sand into the face of the predator—a strategy used by many of the rodents with kangaroo-type legs. (Snakes do not have eyelids—only a thin transparent membrane across the eyes—so this tactic is often successful.)

The color of the wild gerbil is called agouti. In this coloration the individual hairs are banded with yellow, brown, and black. These colors vary in intensity depending upon which region a given gerbil species inhabits. The pattern created provides an excellent camouflage

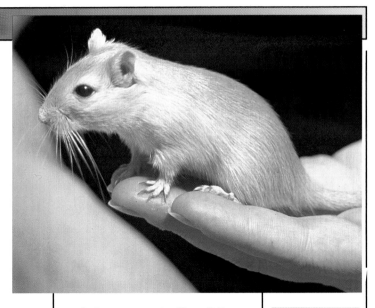

A hand-tame gerbil. Gerbils are not as skittish as are some other types of rodents. In fact, they can be quite friendly once they become accustomed to their keeper and their environment.

Another pleasing characteristic of the gerbil is its curiosity in its surroundings. If something captures a gerbil's attention, the animal will likely investigate it rather than back away.

against the habitat that is made up essentially of sand and rocks, into which the gerbil blends beautifully.

THE EFFECT OF DOMESTICATION

Once any wild animal is bred under captive conditions for many generations, its features will slowly change. The extent of these changes are seen more in the higher mammals, which have greater intelligence, than in rodents. The desire to escape captivity decreases, as does the animal's natural fear of humans. The gerbil bred from generations of domestic stock will stress far less easily than the first generations of gerbils taken from the wild. Of the animals studied in relation to the consequences of domestication, such as dogs, cats, and pigs, there is also evidence that reproduction declines when compared to the wild examples of the species. This is why many domestic animals eventually start to have breeding problems. There is no loss, however, in the intelligence of domesticated species, which appear to channel their intelligence into aspects of domestication. The gerbil, like so many other small rodents, has not been extensively studied in the wild, so there are still many aspects of its life that remain to be unraveled. Under domestic conditions, the chances of mutations surviving are much better than in the wild. As a result, another effect of domestication is that the number of color and fur types begins to steadily increase. This tends to increase the number of people who take up an interest in the species, and this in turn further increases the chances that even more mutations will appear. A species thus gains status as a pet or as a species of commercial importance to us humans.

The Gerbil Hobby

There are several basic reasons why you may wish to keep gerbils. For most hobbyists, it will be as a pet. However, once you have owned a few gerbils, you may decide that you wish to go to the next logical stage, which will be to breed these little animals. Having become a breeder, you may then decide to try your hand at exhibiting your best specimens.

Once you have gained experience as a breeder/exhibitor, you will no doubt find that certain colors have special appeal to you, so you may then decide to breed for them only. There is one final broad area of interest in the gerbil fancy: a number of breeders are now obtaining examples of gerbil species other than the Mongolian gerbil.

The gerbil is an ideal pet because it is possible to keep both sexes together—as long as you are prepared to cope with the numerous offspring that will result. Unlike the hamster, gerbils are very sociable little creatures. They will live happily in a community situation, assuming their accommodations are large enough to reduce the risk of squabbling.

The reproductive capacity of gerbils is high, so they are not difficult to breed. However, advance to this stage only after giving the matter considerable thought. This is because lots of other pet owners also breed large numbers of these pets. The result is that you may have difficulty in disposing of the surplus youngsters. If you decide to become a breeder, it is actually much better that you specialize in the colors

Gerbils can be kept in pairs and in fact enjoy each other's companion-ship. (Of course, if you are keeping members of the opposite sex, you will be faced with caring for the numerous gerbil babies that will result.)

A pair of gerbils at play. Gerbils are amusing little animals that will delight you with their antics.

that are less commonly seen and that will thus have a more ready market, either as pets or as potential breeding and exhibition stock.

Breeding and exhibition types will need to be of good quality, so it may be the case that you will not breed from your initial pet stock but will seek out better quality examples that will form the basis of a good foundation stud.

If you decide to go beyond the pet stage of keeping gerbils,

mice and hamsters; but it is steadily growing with each year. As more color mutations appear and more color combinations are created, the interest in a given pet species increases.

Another aspect of keeping small rodents such as gerbils and mice is developing miniature ecosystems in which they can live. This is a fascinating part of the hobby that allows you to observe these animals in a more natural setting than is

you are certainly advised to join your national gerbil society. You will receive regular newsletters that give information on many interesting topics—and news of forthcoming exhibitions.

The gerbil fancy is, of course, much smaller than that for rabbits, or even

normally seen in the confines of average accommodations. A modification of this theme is creating a gerbil village, complete with little houses and roads. It is akin to the very popular pastime of novelty aquariums in fishkeeping circles.

Housing

Housing arrangements for gerbils can be divided into two basic types: that which is commercially made especially for small rodents, and that which incorporates an aquarium tank as the basic housing unit.

space if more than two gerbils are to be housed in them. There are many designs available, each differing somewhat in size, quality, and the features of the cage. As with most things, you will get what you pay for, and it is

Pet shops stock a variety of cages designed for small rodents such as gerbils. As far as cage size is concerned, the bigger the better.

COMMERCIAL CAGES

Cages for small rodents such as gerbils are readily available in pet shops. The better examples of them are fine for one or two gerbils but will be rather short on

certainly worthwhile purchasing the largest and finest cage you can afford.

Some cages have an all-metal base to which removable chromium bars are fitted. The problem with

this design is that the metal is cold, but, more important, it tends to rust due to the urine of the gerbils. Much better are the modern designs that feature a plastic base that can be totally detached from the chrome cage cover. This allows you to thoroughly clean the floor area. Always check on the quality of the chromium plating because the less expensive models will soon start to rust.

Gerbils will often rub their snouts on the cage bars; and if the chrome is not easily kept clean, this can result in sores. It is also a means by which a health problem can be passed from one gerbil to another. Never purchase a secondhand gerbil cage because you cannot be sure if a diseased animal was the former resident.

The cage may or may not come complete with a sleeping box and a small raised platform that is reached via a ladder. If there is no sleeping box, one can easily be made from some thin wood or by using a plastic container in which a suitably sized hole is made. The box should be large enough for the residents to sleep in comfort—but it does not need to be excessively large. The cage may feature a water bottle and a feeding pot; but if not, these items, along with exercise wheels and other extras, can be purchased from your local pet shop.

A second type of gerbil housing is in the form of a series of interconnecting plastic tubes and drum-shaped containers. It is an attempt to create a more natural housing system for small rodents. It also has the merit of having been designed so that you can continue adding tubes and chambers after you have purchased the basic kit. On the negative side, the basic kit is hardly large enough

Modular units such as this one are designed so that you can add on to them. They come in various shapes and sizes.

This wooden toy serves two purposes: it enables the gerbil to exercise and to satisfy his need to gnaw. Additionally, the mini tunnel simulates the tunnels of gerbils in the wild.

to be regarded as a suitable home—thus extra parts are needed from the outset. Keeping this system clean is not as easy as with a conventional cage. If you can afford the basic kit and some extra parts, it is a nice system; if you cannot, then a large regular hamster cage would be the wiser choice. With the tube/container system, be careful that your gerbils

don't become obese because they just might get stuck in one of the tubes!

THE CONVERTED AQUARIUM

A far better home for your gerbils would be an aquarium, which offers a much greater choice in size and is extremely easy to keep clean. The top must, of course, be covered to prevent the gerbils' escaping. This can be done by using a bird-cage front that has been trimmed to

size, by using a thick metal gauze, or by using heavy wire screening. Each of them can be secured by being held in place with a heavy object. An aquarium canopy can also be used and can feature blue fluorescent lighting to give an interesting effect at night.

Choose the largest aquarium that you can afford as it will provide much greater scope for furnishings.

THE INDIVIDUALLY DESIGNED ECOSYSTEM

If you would like to have a housing arrangement that is a little different from the norm and that provides more room and interest for your gerbils, why not design your own ecosystem? This is a fascinating area of interest because its potential scope is unlimited. You can fashion it so that you can continually add to it.

The basic unit would be a good-sized aquarium made of clear thermoplastic or its equivalent. Carefully cut a hole in one or both ends and then glue clear length, depending on the available space. By utilizing the height (via raised levels) within the system, the total floor area can be increased dramatically. This allows you to "furnish" each area

plastic tubes over the holes. The tubes can then be attached to another aquarium-type unit. Raised levels can be featured—using thermoplastic panels—and can be accessed via a suitably wide and inclined ramp.

The number of gerbils to be housed will determine the number of sleeping cabins that are featured in the design. The overall extensions to the system can be via height, depth, or in a different way. One might be essentially desert, using a mixture of sand, coarse sawdust, and pebbles as the base covering. Another area might contain numerous small logs and rocks. Small potted wild plants that are safe to eat can be included. Some of them may prove a useful fresh source of greenfoods that can easily be replaced if the gerbils destroy or devour them.

To make an interesting

The size of the housing unit depends on the number of gerbils that you intend to keep. If gerbils are overcrowded, they are quite likely to fight—despite their normally pleasant natures.

Facing page: A cinnamon gerbil playing atop its ladder. With the wide array of cage toys that are available, there is no reason for your gerbil to ever be bored.

backdrop, the back panels of the complex could be covered with the kind of aquarium murals that are available from pet stores. The addition of select lighting can be used to superb effect in creating a nighttime look for a particular scene.

The specially designed ecosystem just discussed enables you to observe your pets under conditions that are far different from those of the average pet-cage. Your pets will be more interesting, more natural in their actions, and you may even learn things about them that is not presently known.

Such an undertaking will, of course, require that you pay special attention to hygiene, but the increased area provided will mean that the complex will not get dirty as quickly as will a small cage.

THE BREEDING ROOM

The breeder will obviously need quite a bit of space in which to house a growing stud of gerbils. Most gerbil breeders usually use a shed. If it has utilities connected, they will prove extremely beneficial in attending to day-to-day chores, especially on those dark, cold winter nights. When planning a breeding room,

always try to allow for more room than you think you will need. Once a breeding program is underway, you will find that you will add stock, and all that it entails, at a rapid rate. Space is invariably the first thing that becomes in short supply. Overcrowding will greatly increase the risk of health problems.

Shelves will be needed to accommodate your breeding cages, and an ample work area will be needed as well. Be sure that the breeding-room layout enables you to clean all surfaces with ease. Insulating the walls will help to keep the shed warm in the winter and cool in the summer. The room should be light and airy because harmful bacteria generally will not flourish under such conditions. However, arrange the cages so that none of them are subjected to intense direct sunlight, which might make the gerbils uncomfortably hot, especially in the summer. Ventilation ducts will ensure a good circulation of fresh air. Be sure they are covered with a suitably fine mesh that will prevent wild mice, other rodents, or snakes from entering. All food should be stored in airtight containers—never left in open-top boxes or bags.

It is advisable to purchase one of the many models of ionizers now available. They will remove much bacteria and dust from the breeding room. They are inexpensive to run and should be left on continually. The model the floor or other surfaces, where they are easily wiped away during regular cleaning operations. Ionizers will reduce odors in the process. If your pet shop does not stock them, you can purchase them from specialist bird

must be suitable for the area it is to cover—or you can purchase two smaller ones to achieve the same effect. Ionizers work by releasing millions of negative ions that cling to positive ions, such as dust or bacteria. The increased weight of the particles formed means they fall to suppliers who advertise in the cage-bird magazines.

The breeding room should contain a number of spare cages that can be used on a rotational basis. It is very worthwhile to periodically thoroughly clean and disinfect each cage and then leave it empty in a sunny location for a few weeks. This reduces the opportunity for pathogens to establish a foothold in any of the

cages. All cages should be numbered, and all of their respective food and water containers should carry the same number. This ensures that during refilling and after cleaning, the containers are placed back into the same cage—yet another little aspect of sound health husbandry.

You are advised to have a number of exercise cages for your stock. The number will reflect the number of gerbils being kept. In general, the pet gerbil is given ample time out of its cage. This is normally not so with breeding stock, yet it is these very individuals that should be in the peak of fitness.

Sometimes breeders, in their enthusiasm to produce more and better gerbils, tend to forget the

day-to-day life of their stock. If you are to derive pleasure from your hobby, every effort should be made to ensure that the gerbils enjoy the arrangement as well, and they cannot if they are imprisoned in a small cage all of their lives. As a breeder, you should also ensure that you have the time to devote to each gerbil that you own. If you do not have the time to monitor feeding and spend at least a few minutes watching each individual, then you have too many gerbils and should take measures to reduce the numbers to a more manageable level.

A breeder should allot space for a quarantine area. It should be situated well away from the main stock. If you were also to become an exhibitor, it is advisable that the show stock should also be apart from the main breeding stock, again as a general health-maintenance procedure. You will also need one or more hospital cages.

While some form of heating may be of benefit to you during the winter months, do not keep the temperature too hot. Given a well-insulated breeding room and sufficient bedding material in which your stock can sleep, your gerbils will not normally need any additional heating.

FLOOR COVERING AND BEDDING MATERIAL

There are numerous options for you to select from in terms of floor and bedding materials, each having its advantages and disadvantages.

1. Sawdust. This soaks up urine better than most other materials and is normally free of pathogens when purchased. It is, however, dusty. Apart from getting into the gerbil's eyes and causing an irritation, it can likewise irritate the respiratory system. It also tends to cling to moist foods such as fruit and mashes. Choose larger grades—the sawdust should be coarse—that come from untreated white woods.

2. Woodshavings. While not such a problem in relation to being irritants, shavings are not as absorbent as sawdust. Sometimes the sharp points on hard shavings may

Wood-shavings are one of several floor covering and bedding materials that you can use. They should always be purchased from your pet dealer and never from a lumberyard: those from the latter source have not been sanitized and may carry contaminants.

A hand-tame gerbil is a pleasure to own. Frequent handling and talking to your pet will help build his trust in you.

create minor eye injuries in young gerbils.

3. Sand. Although a very natural surface for gerbils, sand is, nonetheless, rather abrasive. It also clings to food items and may stain the fur of light-colored varieties. The coarser grades are better than the finer ones.

4. Soil. Again, this is a very natural surface for gerbils, but it may contain the eggs and larvae of parasites, as well as being home to many pathogens. You can bake it to ensure that it is sterile if you especially would like to use it. You can also purchase baked clays that are commercially prepared for aquarists.

5. Straw. This is not a very good medium for either floor covering or bedding. It is not very absorbent, and its sharp edges represent a definite injury risk to adult and young stock alike.

6. Hay. This is absorbent if enough is used, and it makes excellent bedding. It it is also a nutritious food, so it is very popular with all rodent keepers. It must be fresh; otherwise, it will be a breeding ground for pathogens and parasites. It must also be replaced daily so that there is no chance that in its dampened form (from urine) it becomes a pathogenic paradise. Do not use hay for breeding females as it can generate too much heat for the newly born infants.

7. Granulated paper. This commercially made floor covering is excellent as it has high absorbency and does not stick to foods quite as readily as does sawdust. It is, however, more costly.

8. Commercial bedding.

floor of the accommodations should also feature a few variably sized twigs from fruit trees. They will be bene-ficial

Special fiber bedding is now made for rodents and offers good hygiene-quality, combined with excellent insulation properties.

Do not use wool, nylon wool, or wood wools, as each of them are potentially fatal to small rodents like gerbils. If swallowed, they may cause an internal blockage. Wood wools (used in packaging) can strangle small gerbils if they get entangled around the animals' necks. Usually, hobbyists will use a combination of the recommended materials, such as a sawdust base with some wood shavings or a paper base with sawdust and shavings. A few dried leaves will be appreciated by gerbils; choose those from fruit trees or others that you know are nontoxic. The in providing your pets with something upon which they can gnaw, which is very important to all rodents and lagomorphs (rabbits and hares). You can also include wooden spools as they will be useful play items. Empty toilet tissue holders will also be gnawed and will provide your gerbils with a play toy that is easily replaced.

Avoid thin-plastic toys because if they are gnawed, small pieces may be swallowed, with possibly fatal consequences. The same applies to all soft-rubber toys. If you feature an exercise wheel in your pet's cage, purchase one that is of solid, rather than barred, construction. Doing so will prevent the possibility of the gerbil getting its tail caught up in the rungs of the wheel.

Be careful with toys that are made of plastic. If the plastic isn't thick and durable, your gerbil may be able to nibble away tiny fragments that can lodge in his stomach and possibly kill him.

Selecting Your Gerbil

Right: A black gerbil about to chow down. The most important concern when choosing a gerbil is the animal's state of health. All other considerations are secondary.

Facing page: A healthy gerbil should have bright clear eyes with no evidence of discharge. The nose should be dry and clean, and the ears should be erect.

The first priority when purchasing any pet is that it should be a very healthy specimen. This is especially important with small animals such as gerbils because they are not easily treated should they become ill. Fortunately, gerbils do not seem to suffer with quite the number of problems that are seen in mice and hamsters, which is one good reason for choosing them as pets. Of course, a breeder is more likely to meet with problems simply because larger numbers of these pets are kept within a relatively small area. It then becomes a matter of being extremely diligent in matters of hygiene.

Other than in relation to the health of potential purchases, you will need to consider a number of other aspects, depending on whether you are looking simply for nice pets or possible breeding stock.

FIRST IMPRESSIONS COUNT

When purchasing pet gerbils, the first thing to bear in mind is that first impressions are often important. This is especially so in relation to the conditions under which the gerbils are being kept by the seller. The premises should be very clean, as should the cages or other forms of housing. If the accommodations show evidence that they are not cleaned too often, the best thing to do is locate another supplier. An excess of fecal droppings, dirty water bottles, cracked food bowls, and dirt on the panels of the aquariums that house small animals are all indications that the

seller does not devote a lot of attention to the general welfare of his stock.

Likewise, if one or more of the gerbils on display shows evidence of a problem, this is hardly an encouraging sign for you. The chances are that the rest of the stock will soon fall victim to the same problems.

THE HEALTHY GERBIL

If you are satisfied with the conditions under which the gerbils are being kept, you should then observe them as they move around. You are looking for any that may show some form of restriction in their movements. Restricted movement could be the result of a minor strain,

An assortment of variously colored gerbils. Before selecting your gerbil, you should closely observe his behavior. Do not buy a gerbil that does not respond to activity in his environment.

but it may also be of a genetic base that will not correct itself. Assuming that all the stock looks sound, you should then ask the seller to let you inspect one or two gerbils that appeal to you in terms of their colors.

Start the inspection with the head. The eyes should be round and express lots of vitality; they should not be dull. They should be quite clear, with no signs of weeping. The same is true of the nostrils, which should show no signs of a liquid discharge or mucus. The nose should be dry to just slightly damp—never wet. The ears are short, unwrinkled, and erect. The teeth of the upper jaw should just touch those of the lower jaw: this ensures that they will wear away in an even manner. Should they be out of alignment, they will continue to grow

and cause problems for the gerbil when it eats. While they can be periodically trimmed by your vet, it is better not to have the problem in the first place. Certainly any gerbils that are found to have defective teeth alignment should never be used for breeding as the problem will be inherited by their offspring.

The coat of a gerbil should be sleek and should exhibit obvious vitality. Any bald areas   indicate a definite problem. Fortunately, rodents rarely suffer from lice or flea infestations unless their accommodations are in a really bad state. You should, therefore, never see evidence of parasitic infestation: dark brown or red specks, which are the fecal droppings of fleas and lice.

The gerbil has five digits on each of its feet. Although a missing digit will not affect a gerbil, it would render an exhibition prospect valueless. Check the anal region below the root of the tail. It should be quite clean, with no fecal matter

congealed in the fur. Staining in the anal region would suggest a present or recent problem with diarrhea. The tail should be straight, with no kinks in it. Poor tail condition will not affect the general health of a pet gerbil, but it would be a major fault in a breeding or show specimen.

you select females as they tend to be less quarrelsome than males. If you select one or more of each sex, you will be presented with a number of babies in due course, so it is best to initially stick with one sex or the other. The seller will advise you of the gerbils' sex, but you can check this out in the following manner: The distance between the anus and the genitals is

Either sex can make a good pet. If you are planning to keep several gerbils, it is a good idea to choose females as they generally tend to be less quarrelsome than males.

In a potential show specimen, the tail should have good size at its root and should steadily taper to a well-rounded tip. Good tail length is also needed in a potential breeding specimen. The tail should be covered with a generous coating of hair that forms a very slight brush at the tip.

WHICH SEX?

Either sex will make an ideal pet. If you wish to keep a few gerbils together, it is probably better that

greater in the male than in the female. Further, the scrotal sacs will be evident in a male once it is about four or more weeks of age.

WHAT AGE TO PURCHASE?

Gerbils are weaned from their mother's milk when they are about three weeks of age, so they can go to their new homes any time after the age of three weeks. Probably an age of four to five weeks is best as this should ensure that the youngsters are fully independent. The average lifespan of a gerbil will be on the order of three or so years, but some individuals may attain five years. It is thus best to obtain young stock, which will also be more readily tamed. However, even adults that have received little handling quickly become hand tame.

HOW MANY TO PURCHASE?

Gerbils are social animals so they are best kept in pairs or small groups, providing the accommodations are large enough for the latter. Once a group has been established, additions to it are more risky. Some individuals will be accepted without problem while others will be bullied, so it is best to establish a small group of youngsters from the outset.

WILL GERBILS MIX WITH OTHER RODENTS?

The short answer to this is no. If baby mice are brought up with similarly aged gerbils they will get along very well, but the mixing of different rodent species is not recommended. Hamsters, for example, are rather solitary creatures and possess more than just a trace of belligerence in the make-up. They will quickly fight with gerbils. Keep all rodent pets only with their own kind.

SELECTING BREEDING AND EXHIBITION STOCK

If you plan to breed and exhibit gerbils, the procedure for obtaining stock will be somewhat different from that of purchasing pet specimens. This is because you really need to know something about the ancestors of the first gerbils that you acquire. Further, they must be very sound examples of the species; otherwise, you will be devoting a lot of needless time to the process of upgrading quality.

Gerbils are weaned at about three weeks of age, but it is best to purchase them when they are four to five weeks of age: by this time they will be completely independent.

Good breeding and show stock is fortunately not expensive in small rodents as it is in larger pets, so there is no need to commence with anything other than good examples. The best thing to do is to try and visit a gerbil or small rodent exhibition first. At such affairs you will see most, if not all, of the available colors. You will also be able to chat with many breeders.

Find one that is breeding winning stock but at a level that suits your budget. Some may sell stock that has already won some awards and has produced quality youngsters. Alternatively, you may purchase the offspring of a winning pair. They will be less expensive, but, of course, their quality (or lack of it) will not be evident for some months. I would opt for a proven pair or a trio of one male and two females. This way you can see what you are getting rather than purchasing in the hopes the younger stock will mature into good breeding examples.

By viewing a goodly number of exhibition examples, you will be much more aware of what a really

Head study of a gerbil. Gerbil ownership is not a costly venture. Even good breeding stock and show-quality specimens are moderately priced.

nice gerbil should look like in terms of both conformation and color. If possible, try to locate a breeder that is in your area because you can then visit his home to see the rest of his stock. A good breeder will maintain written breeding records, and the stock not being exhibited will be almost as good as that which is.

Some breeders rely on a hit-or-miss type of program in order to obtain a few show specimens; others strive to achieve a high standard of consistency throughout their stock. It is the latter breeder from whom you should purchase. In such an instance, you should obtain all of your initial stock from the same breeder. If you purchase from different breeders and crossbreed their lines, many years of careful breeding could be negated at the very first generation of youngsters. In any form of livestock breeding, the object is to try and improve the stock at each generation by removing faults and fixing in virtues. This is only possible if a breeder stays within a given gene pool and does not randomly mix bloodlines, unless a specific need to do this is called for. If you have a strong desire to work with a specific color, seek out a breeder who specializes in this color. You will find that the more you specialize, the greater will be your chances of success. This is because you will need to retain quite a few of the initial offspring that you produce (assuming they are of the needed standard). This is rarely possible if you attempt to breed a number of varieties.

Do not attempt to commence with too many gerbils. For one thing, you may tire of the hobby after a short while, as many newcomers do. However, even if you gain in enthusiasm, it is prudent to develop your line slowly, based on sound knowledge. This can only come about with the passage of time. Your initial stock may not prove quite what you had hoped for, so there may be a need to restart the whole program with all, or at least some, stock from another breeder. These facts make a steady development the wisest way to proceed.

You may find it worthwhile to develop two quite separate lines of stock on the basis that if one fails to meet your hopes, the other may prove a success. It also affords you the opportunity to use each line as an outcross to the other.

Feeding Gerbils

Gerbils are discriminating eaters. They will carefully sniff their food before eating it.

The gerbil is an extremely easy little animal to care for in terms of its nutritional needs. Even so, you will be more able to rodents, the gerbil is very cosmopolitan in what it will eat—one of the reasons why this group of animals has proved so successful.

ensure that it receives the ideal diet if you have some basic understanding of the varying roles of food in the body. This will enable you to plan a feeding regimen that is nutritionally balanced yet interesting to your pets. Like all other

The rodent digestive system evolved to cope with foods of a plant source, so such foods form the basis of the diet. However, some foods of animal origin are important because they contain certain ingredients not found in plant foods.

Commercial food mixes, available from pet shops, contain cereal and seeds and are fortified with vitamins.

The wild rodent would normally obtain them in the form of insects, their eggs and larvae, as well as via other invertebrates, such as worms. An amount of carrion will also be eaten should it come a rodent's way, though whether or not this is applicable to the gerbil is not known. Before discussing the diet in more detail, we will first look at other aspects of feeding.

FOOD CONTAINERS

The ideal food containers will be those made of crock (earthenware). They are not easily knocked over by your pet, as are those made of

plastic or aluminum. You can purchase small ones suitable for gerbils, mice, and hamsters. One will be required for seed, and one will be needed for soft foods. Water is best

supplied via gravity-fed bottles fitted with metal nozzles. They are available in a suitable size from your pet store. They are hung from the cage bars. If your gerbil's home is a converted aquarium, you will need to fashion a means of suspending the bottle so that it is within reach of the gerbils yet is secure.

WHEN TO FEED

It is not important at what specific hour you feed your gerbils as long as they are fed at the same time every day. Apart from this is the fact that dry foods such as seeds, as well as water, should always be available to them—so they will never actually go hungry. Soft foods such as fruits and mashes are best supplied in the early evening. This allows the gerbils plenty of time overnight—when they are most active—to consume such foods at their leisure. Uneaten soft foods can then be removed the following morning so that they do not spoil during the warmer part of the day.

HOW MUCH TO FEED

In the wild, a gerbil will expend quite a lot of energy foraging for food. This fact, together with the limited supply of food items in the gerbil's natural habitat, ensures that it will not become obese. The situation is rather different for pets, which not only have a more restricted activity level but also have a much wider range of foods at their disposal. This being so, you must monitor your gerbils' food so that substances such as proteins and fats are not given so liberally as to cause obesity. Should this become apparent, you must not suddenly cut off the food supply in order that your pets can shed a little weight.

It is also important when feeding any animal that it should never be fed a glut of a given food. This invariably induces stomach upset, with resultant diarrhea (also known as scours). This is most applicable to soft food and vegetable items containing a high water content. Always introduce these foods on a gradual basis until the desired level is reached. Any new food should be introduced slowly so that you can monitor its effects on your pets.

UNSUITABLE FOODS

Never feed your pets any foods that are grown from

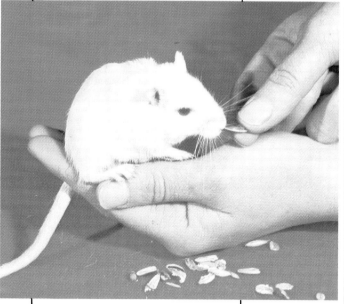

bulbs as they are poisonous to gerbils. This also applies to many wild plants so try to become familiar with those found in your locality if you plan to include wild plants in your gerbil's diet. The twigs and bark of some trees and shrubs also fall into the undesirable category so the best course of action is not to supply an item if you are not sure of its status. Sweet items such as candies are obviously not foods that should be given to any pet as they will damage its teeth as badly as they will your own. The *occasional* tidbit of cookie or cake may be given as a treat. Never feed any food item that is not fresh. Be especially wary of high-fat-content seeds that have split open. They will exude

Sunflower seeds are a favored food item of gerbils, but they should not be fed in large quantities because they are fattening.

a toxic liquid. Bedding hay, which is a very good food, should always be fresh, never moldy or damp. Be wary of foods gathered from gardens that may have been treated with pesticides. Always wash fruits and vegetables before feeding them to your pets.

A good diet provides the fuel that your gerbil needs for playing and other activities.

together with mashes to which a liquid has been added. Dry foods will be seeds, grain, and nuts, together with bread, biscuits, and other similar items.

Other than in the amount of moisture that a food contains, the essential constituents are proteins, fats, and carbohydrates. Additionally, all foods contain various vitamins and minerals. Though not foods in themselves, these substances are nonetheless crucial to the existence of all animal life forms.

MAJOR FOOD CONSTITUENTS

All foods can be broadly categorized into one of three types based on their constituents. They can then be divided into those that have a high water content and those that have one that is lower. A balanced diet will contain foods of various water contents: fruits, vegetables,

Proteins. The basic role of proteins in metabolism is that they serve as the building blocks of the body. Muscle and other tissues are essentially composed of proteins—as is the blood. After water, the next most common substance in the body is protein in its many forms. Proteins are made up of different chemical compounds known as amino acids. They are found in all foods, but certain essential ones are found only in animal tissue, which is why some animal-origin foods are needed by gerbils.

When proteins are oxidized in the body, they are broken down into their constituent amino acids and then rebuilt into the kind of tissues needed by the animal. Young gerbils, together with breeding females, need a larger quantity of proteins than does the average non-breeding adult. A gerbil recovering from an illness also needs extra proteins because while it was ill it will have broken down muscle tissue to nourish itself.

Excess proteins in the diet will be converted to fatty tissue and can also be used as an energy food. Fortunately, the total amount of foods that a pet gerbil will eat is small, so the only reason a pet owner might need to monitor the ration of proteins supplied is in order to ensure that the gerbils do not become obese.

High-protein foods of plant origin include the following: sunflower, safflower, linseed, rape, maw, niger, all nuts (break large ones into pieces that the gerbils can cope with), kidney beans, lentils, and soybeans. No fruits have a high-protein content but dried apricots, dried figs, and dried dates have much more protein than most other fruits. Likewise, vegetables are not protein rich, though unripe peas, together with broccoli and spinach, contain more than other popular vegetables. Of the foods that are of animal origin, there are numerous ones that are rich in proteins. They include the following: cheese, dried non-fat milk, powdered egg, and to a lesser extent raw egg yolk. Meats themselves, whether of cattle, poultry or fish, are obviously rich in protein, as are beef extracts.

This gerbil obviously receives a well-balanced diet as evidenced by its beautiful shiny coat. Proteins, fats, and carbohydrates are the major food constituents, and each has its own important role in keeping your gerbil healthy.

Fats. These compounds serve numerous functions of which insulation is high on the list. Fatty tissue provides the internal

Apples are one of several fruits that your pet will eat with relish. Gerbils enjoy variety in their diet so keep this in mind when preparing your pet's meals.

organs with protection from buffering, as well as insulation from the cold. This should not be a major need in pets kept under domestic conditions. Fat is crucial in providing taste to different foods, as well as being the means by which fat-soluble vitamins are transported in the body. Fat-rich plant foods include the seeds already listed because fat is invariably found in association with protein. Animal-origin fats include those listed under protein, plus items such as butter, lard, olive and cod liver oils, which are all essentially made up of fats.

Carbohydrates. These compounds are sugars in their various forms. Their main role in metabolism is to provide a readily available source of energy for muscle activity. They also provide bulk to the diet and are utilized in many other metabolic reactions. The source of carbohydrates for most pet animals will be in the form of either seeds or cereal products. They include the following: Wheat, millet in its numerous forms, canary seed, maize, bran, breakfast cereals, bread, and dog biscuits. Other items, such as dried apricots and soybeans, are also rich in carbohydrates. Even fruits such as apple, grapes, dates, and bananas have a relatively high carbohydrate content when compared with fruits such as strawberries or melons.

Vitamins. These compounds provide the body with protection against disease. There are many vitamins and each plays its own role in the overall health of your gerbils. They are found mainly in fruits and green plants, though all foods contain some vitamins—albeit in smaller quantities when compared to fruits. Vitamin A is important to all animals, and rich sources include dried apricots, cherries, and peaches. Carrots are also a useful source of this vitamin.

Wild plants such as dandelion, chickweed, parsley, and shepherd's purse will be enjoyed according to individual taste and are good sources of various vitamins, as are beet tops, cress, spinach, and tomatoes. All foods contain the various minerals needed by the body, so you should never have a problem concerning them if a varied diet is supplied. However, during the breeding period, a female may benefit from a little extra calcium, either in the form of a powder sprinkled onto moist foods or via bread soaked in milk.

Some breeders add vitamin supplements to the food of their stock, but caution is advised in this practice. The ratio of one vitamin to another is of some importance because an excess of one may negatively affect the absorption of another. Some vitamins can be stored in the body (in the liver); others cannot, so the indiscriminate use of supplements is definitely not recommended—especially if your pets

of small mammals such as gerbils, hamsters, mice, and rats. They contain cereals, seed, and other items and are fortified with vitamins.

MASHES

Mashes are merely mixtures of various items that are blended together and lightly moistened. The advantage of a mash is that it ensures that your pet does not pick out all of the favored items—which may not necessarily be those that are most beneficial to him. The basis of a mash can be a breakfast cereal into which egg, meat stock, fruits, seeds, and other items are blended. It should be just damp, not mushy. A mash will not stay fresh for any great length of time so always remove any leftovers after a few hours have passed.

GERMINATED SEEDS

If you would like to make a few seeds more appetizing for your gerbils, you might try soaking them in tepid water for about 24 hours. In this form, they will be enjoyed by all of the stock, and they are especially beneficial to young or ailing gerbils. The soaking prompts the seeds to

Greenfoods such as lettuce can be offered to your gerbil, but keep the portions small. Too much of any greenfood can cause diarrhea.

receive a varied diet. Only if you suspect that your gerbils are lacking overall health and vitality should you consider supplements and then only after consulting your veterinarian. The problem may not be one of a lack of vitamins.

COMMERCIAL FOODS

There is a variety of pre-packaged food mixtures from which you can choose. These products are specially formulated to meet the nutritional needs commence the germination process. The vitamin content rises, and the seeds are more easily digested. Once soaked, they must be thoroughly rinsed in fresh water. They have a limited life in this form, so remove any uneaten seeds after a few hours. If they are allowed to germinate, the young shoots will also be eaten by your pets; but *do not give them shoots that have grown very long*. To germinate the seeds, they will need to be soaked for about 48 hours. Place them in a darkened cupboard for soaking and germinating. If they fail to germinate, this indicates that the seeds are not of good quality.

GENERAL GUIDELINES

Of the various foods discussed, you can see that there are few foods that your gerbil cannot be offered. As a rule of thumb, you can assume that if you can eat it, so can your gerbil. If it is not an item that is regarded as being healthy for humans, it probably isn't for your pets either. You will find that gerbils are as variable in their tastes as we humans are. Take note of which foods are readily accepted and which are not. You will learn by trial and error which foods are most appreciated. By the same process, you will know what quantities of foods should be given per day.

It is very important that you observe your gerbils when they are eating. By so doing you will know if they are picky eaters or those that eat with great relish. This knowledge can be important: any change in eating behavior may be the first (and only) sign that you may get that a gerbil is feeling unwell. At such times, it is crucial that he continues to eat, so knowing what his favorite items are can be very important.

A pair of agouti, or wild-colored, gerbils.

The Pet Gerbil

Before actually purchasing your pet gerbils, it is advisable to first obtain housing for them. Doing so will prevent your rushing around at the last minute and purchasing items that are not quite seeds—so that your pets can nibble on something. Once home, place the gerbils in their accommodations and let them explore. Supply them with seeds, water, and maybe a few small

Have everything ready for your pet before you bring him home. Once he has settled in, leave him alone and let him explore his new surroundings.

what you had in mind. Once you have the cage and its furnishings on hand, you can then devote your attention to obtaining the gerbils of your color choice.

The seller will supply you with a cardboard box in which you can transport your pets home. Place some sawdust and hay in the box, as well as a few

pieces of fruit. The cage should be positioned so that they can see you as you move around. It must be protected from direct sunlight so that they will not become overheated. Additionally, it should be placed where cats or other pets cannot look into it, which would obviously frighten its occupants.

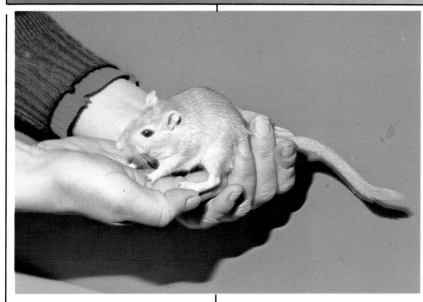

This is the correct way to handle a gerbil: secure the root of the tail with the thumb and index finger of one hand and support the body with the other hand.

HANDLING GERBILS

Gerbils, along with some other rodents, can be very friendly little creatures, especially if they are acquired at a young age. Unlike hamsters, which have no tails to speak of, gerbils do, so they are really easy to handle. When lifting up a gerbil, simply grasp the root of its tail between your index finger and thumb and then lift its rear end up. This allows you to slide your hand under its body in order to support its weight. In this position, a gerbil will be quite content and secure, and you can then release hold of its tail. However, you may need to retain hold of young gerbils during their first few days of being handled, just in case they become frightened and jump. On landing, they could easily break a leg or sustain other injuries.

Once your gerbils are quite familiar with your hand, you will be able to just lift them up without any problems. *Be sure that you grasp the root and not the tip or another part of the tail, and do support the body with your free hand.* It is very important that young children are shown the correct way to handle your new pets; otherwise, they may hurt them, and this will tend to make the gerbils more likely to nip the children's fingers.

You must also strongly emphasize to children that they should not place the gerbils near your pet cat or dog if you have one, or you will probably be short of your gerbils, which are among the natural prey of

Gerbils are energetic little animals. If you have a pair, they will greatly enjoy playing with each other.

these predators. Likewise, children should be supervised when they are playing with gerbils that have been let out of their cage—just in case they lose them. This is not an uncommon happening.

you can do is to leave some food nearby: when they eventually come out for it, hopefully you will have the opportunity to capture them.

Alternatively, leave their cage (opened) nearby so that they can gain entry into it. They may become frightened at their freedom; and if so, they will be more than happy to return to the security of their little home.

SAFETY MEASURES

Being such small animals, gerbils can very easily get lost in the average home once they are taken out of their cage. In such a situation, it is prudent to check around the edges of your walls and in floorboards to see that there are no holes from which the pets might exit the room. If there are no holes, this means that the gerbils at least cannot venture too far—other than through open doors. In a kitchen, they may scurry under a refrigerator or similar appliances that are not easily moved. In this situation, the only thing

GERBIL INTELLIGENCE

Gerbils, like most other rodents, are very inquisitive creatures. They are actually quite intelligent for their small size, but they cannot apply reason to solve problems. Nonetheless, by reacting to a combination of positive and negative stimuli and by the use of their powers of memory recall, they are able to learn to do many things.

They will display their intelligence in the obvious

pleasure they will derive from running in and out of tubes, by rolling bobbins, and in their mock fighting. They will greatly enjoy being stroked and handled once they have become really tame and will sit on their rear haunches in order to take tidbits from you.

Because they do possess an active mind, you should give them simple problems to solve, which will help to reduce stress brought about by confinement. Apart from making their accommodations as interesting as possible, you can place certain dry food items among the floor covering material. This simple act of prompting them to use their senses to discover food simulates their situation in the wild. You might also devise ways of suspending or hiding food somewhere in the cage while at the same time keeping it accessible so that the gerbils could get at it if they really tried. If touching a given prompt results in a tidbit falling to the cage floor, they will soon realize that the one action leads to a successful conclusion.

Of course, these kinds of tests must be done with food items that they like, and their regular rations must always be available to them so that there is no risk that they will ever go hungry. Once they succeed in a task, they will easily perform it again and again. It is then a case of thinking up a somewhat more complex problem for them to overcome. By the use of positive stimuli, they can build up a repertoire of actions that might amaze your friends as to their

This gerbil is being trained to go through a maze-like compartment. His owner has hidden a tidbit for him to find.

A playful trio of gerbils. Their owner has provided them with a generous layer of nice fresh wood-shavings, in which they will enjoy burrowing.

intelligence. It is by this means that the large macaws and other parrots are taught to do all of their tricks. Your gerbils are not as intelligent as a parrot, but they might surprise you as to what they can achieve if you are patient and ingenious in the tests that you devise.

INTRODUCING OTHER GERBILS

Although gerbils are quite social animals, this does not mean that you can introduce a new gerbil into the cage of an already resident gerbil without problems arising. This is doubly so if two gerbils are already in residence. They may attack the new gerbil, which they regard as an intruder to their domain. If you do acquire an extra gerbil, it is probably better to put it in a cage that has only one gerbil in it. If the two fight, you must quickly separate them and try again another day. On the second occasion there may be less aggression, and the two may become friends.

The *average* lifespan for a gerbil is about three years, but some gerbils have lived beyond that age.

An alternative (and safer) method is to place the two gerbils in a partitioned cage so that they can see and sniff each other through the partition but not come to blows. You can observe their reaction to each other before letting them meet. Again, if they do not seem to like each other, try again a day or so later. If this still results in fighting, you can assume that you have two incompatible gerbils; and so you should house them separately.

THE OLDER PET

As your gerbils get older you may find that they will start to lose some of their hair. This is a quite normal situation. They will also become less active. In some instances they may develop tumor-like growths. As long as the growths are benign, they will not cause any discomfort to the gerbils. You should let your veterinarian examine your gerbils that evidence these growths: he can check on them and tell you exactly what they are. As noted earlier, when your gerbils reach the age of three years, they are getting close to their average life expectancy. If they have been accommodated in ideal conditions and well looked after, they just *might* go on to see their fifth birthday.

Breeding Gerbils

A litter of ten-day-old gerbils. Their colors are black, cinnamon, dove, and agouti.

While the breeding of gerbils is a fascinating aspect of the hobby, the novice should always ask himself why he wishes to undertake such a project. Simply breeding stock for its own sake has very little merit in this day and age. A factor that is not always taken into account by the average pet owner who decides to breed is that relating to the disposal of surplus stock. There is no shortage of breeders; and whenever this situation prevails, the result is that the price you can expect to get for youngsters will not be equal to your costs in producing them. For most people, it will not mean financial gain. If you do wish to breed gerbils, it therefore makes sense to consider the best way to proceed with the venture. My first piece of advice is that you should not become overly ambitious too early in the program. Keep the project down to a low-profile level that enables you to see if you really do wish to become deeply involved in the hobby. Do not rush out and purchase a number of gerbils just because they are inexpensive. The cost of feeding them will almost certainly exceed their purchase cost over a span of time.

Consider very carefully the fact that as litters are born and reach weaning age, they will need accommodations of their own. You must thus have enough spare cages and the room to house them and other breeding-related items. You must also have time available to devote to feeding, cleaning, and general care of the stock to which you have committed yourself.

BREEDING OBJECTIVES

Once you are certain that you do wish to be a breeder and are prepared to make the necessary investment in time and money to get a program underway, the next thing to do is to consider your objectives. You may wish to become an exhibitor and produce your own show stock or you may wish to specialize in certain colors. Of course you could combine both of these objectives. Either way, your long-term goals will be to steadily improve the color of your gerbils and their quality.

Take the time to visit shows, and study possible breeding room layouts before you commence. The better your planning is the less problems you will encounter. Choose your initial breeding stock with great care because these gerbils will be the foundation to all that follows. Study breeding strategies and

This is the only type of exercise wheel that should be used for gerbils. Its solid-back construction prevents injuries to gerbils' tails.

genetics by obtaining specialty books on these topics—the investment in time and cost will be repaid many times over.

PAIRING GERBILS

You can pair a male with one, two, or three females; but initially, and especially when color breeding, it may be better to have one male to each female. In this way you will not suddenly be overrun with too many youngsters. Gerbils pair for life if allowed to do so. The actual mating ritual commences by the male chasing the

BREEDING CONDITION

Before any gerbils are bred, it is most important that they are in full breeding condition. Not only must they be in a hard, trim physical state but they must also have been prepared nutritionally for reproduction. This is especially important for the female, whose body and strength are obviously drained by the process of pregnancy, birth, and care of the litter. However, as far as the care aspect is concerned, the male will assist in rearing the babies.

The pair should have received ample exercise—which they will get if you have provided a spacious cage for them. The diet can be modified a few weeks prior to the anticipated birth of the litter. The amount of protein

A dove female and an agouti male. At the bottom of the photo is one of their babies of a litter of four.

female around their home until eventually the female stands still and mating occurs. It is quite brief and will be repeated numerous times.

given can be slowly increased, and extra calcium (in powder or milk form) can be supplied. It is essentially for the female; but, of course, the male will eat some as well. This regimen can be maintained throughout the nursing period, after which the gerbils can be slowly returned to their normal rations.

BREEDING FACTS

As previously indicated, the gerbil reaches sexual maturity when about two to three months of age. Once mated, the gestation period (the time between fertilization of sperm and ova, and the birth of offspring) is normally 23 to 27 days. The female estrus, the period when she will allow a male to mate with her, lasts for about four days and cycles every six days. The gerbil can exhibit what is known as delayed implantation after a litter has been born. This means that the day after giving birth to offspring she can remate. The fertilized zygotes will not, however, become implanted into the uterus until her present litter is weaned.

The average litter will comprise five to seven infants, but the range can be as many as ten. The newborn babies are blind, deaf, naked, and helpless. Their fur grows rapidly, and within about a week they are fully furred. Their ears open within a week, and their eyes open when

they are about ten days of age. At this time they may be able to scramble out of their nest. They reach weaning age when about 21 days old; but this can vary a few days, some youngsters being rather slower to be weaned than others. As soon as their eyes are open, young gerbils will actually start to nibble at things, and by the time they are about 14 days of age they will be able to eat quite a number of items.

In theory, a female can give birth to a large number

A pregnant gerbil contentedly nibbling a piece of lettuce. Providing a breeding female with a balanced diet is essential for the health and soundness of her offspring.

A three-day-old gerbil litter. Gerbils are born blind, deaf, and naked.

of litters in a single year, but you should not allow her to do so. This places a great strain on her physique and will ultimately result in a loss of vigor in the offspring. To prevent continued breeding will entail separating the sexes for periods at a time. This will have some other benefits in that it will allow you to control how many offspring you have to cope with at any one period. In order that you do not lose sight of which of your stock are established pairs or trios, you can keep them in adjacent cages or in some way mark the females with an ink spot, so that you know which have mated with which males.

BREEDING PROBLEMS

Normally, gerbils are extremely reliable breeders, but some problems may be occasionally experienced. A first-time mother may become frightened at the sight of her own offspring and kill the first one or two babies born. She may even devour all of the litter. Usually, subsequent litters are born and reared without problem. Obviously, if a gerbil proves to be an unreliable mother, she is best not bred once this fact is established. Her offspring may also become poor mothers. The males likewise can inherit the trait, which they can pass on to any of the daughters that they subsequently sire.

A stressed, very nervous, or underfed female may also devour her own offspring. In order to reduce fear in a female, especially with a first-time mother, do not be tempted to unduly interfere when you know that a litter is imminent. If the nest is to be inspected, this should be done when the female is not in it. Do not handle the babies during the first few days of their life, and rub some of the floor litter on your hands when you do have occasion to pick up the infants. This will reduce your own scent on the youngsters.

When preparing the nest for breeding pairs, you are advised not to use hay, but instead choose one of the commercial rodent-bedding materials. Hay can become very hot. It also presents a big health risk in a nestful of babies, which will dampen it with their urine. This will tend to provide ideal breeding conditions for bacteria at a time when you will not be changing the bedding quite as often as you normally would.

FOSTERING

Should the need arise to foster offspring to other gerbils, this can be done as long as another female has offspring of about the same age. Once again, attend to this matter when the foster parents are away from their nest. Rub some litter soil from the foster parent's cage onto the foster gerbils before placing them in the nest. You might even smear just a little butter on them. This will prompt the parents to wash the infants, and in so doing

A litter of six-day-old gerbils. The size of a gerbil litter averages between five and seven.

they will transfer their own scent onto the babies.

Fostering may be advised when one pair of gerbils have a large litter while another pair have only a small one. If possible, place the offspring into the nest of gerbils of another color. In this way you will not lose track of which youngsters belong to which parents. This will be important for record-keeping purposes.

NURSERY CAGES

When the youngsters are weaned, they should be placed into separate quarters, based on their sex. This will prevent unwanted litters from those individuals that reach sexual maturity at a very early age. If possible, try to avoid placing a single youngster in a cage by itself. Gerbils are social animals and need the company of their own kind. Monitor the first few days very carefully because sometimes a youngster may not be fully independent and may need to be placed back with its parents if they will still accept it. For this reason, it is always wise to be really sure that the offspring are feeding on their own before they are taken from their parents.

RECORDS

You are strongly advised to maintain detailed records of your breeding activities. They will be invaluable to you as time goes by. They will be

A dove female and an agouti Canadian white spot mating.

Gerbils develop very quickly. These 12-day-old youngsters are already fully furred.

helpful in establishing which of your gerbils are best to breed. Each gerbil should have its own record card that details its number, age, color, markings, number of times mated, number of offspring and how many of them lived to reach maturity. Illnesses should also be noted on the card. Additionally you may also note show wins, together with any other data that you feel will be useful in the future.

Breeding cards should also be kept. They should show which gerbils were paired, how many offspring were born and survived, and what their colors and sex were. It is also useful to note their weights at different times during their development.

GRADING OFFSPRING

In order to ensure that your stock steadily improves, it is important that you retain only the very best gerbils for your ongoing breeding program. To accomplish this, you must make judicious selections, and there are many systems that breeders use for doing this. A few considerations are given here—but you should study methods of selection in more detailed breeding books.

1. From the outset, you should obtain an expert opinion, such as from a

show judge, as to the merits and shortcomings of your stock. They should be noted in the order of their importance to you. They will provide the working model against which you will assess improvement. Bear in mind that as you improve one feature another may regress, and it may also change the balance of other features. It is, therefore, extremely difficult to upgrade stock once it has reached a reasonable level of quality. This is why only a very few breeders make it right to the top.

2. Assessing stock needs to be done at different ages as a gerbil matures. A well-colored, good-looking youngster of two months of age may not be so well colored or good when it is six months old. You must also remember that a good-looking gerbil may not pass its looks onto its offspring, so the youngsters must also form part of your grading system to assess which of them are genetically as good as their appearance would suggest.

3. You must decide whether to try and improve the stock one feature at a time or to attain overall improvements at each generation. The former method may bring more rapid results, but regression in other features may also become more apparent.

4. Your judgment must be consistent, so do not get carried away by the sudden appearance of a gerbil that may excel in one feature but shows faults in others. The excessive use of such a gerbil will create a yo-yo effect, and real progress may be inhibited. Having decided what your priorities are, you should have the faith of your own convictions and stick with your intended program so that it has time to be effective.

5. Your priorities will, of course, change as each feature is improved. If you exhibit your stock, success or failure will tell you if your program is working. If you do not exhibit, you will periodically need to have a good exhibitor or judge assess matters.

6. Breeding for both new colors and quality of conformation will prove to be the most challenging of all of your endeavors. This is because, generally, anatomy and color are not linked. It just seems to happen that often a nicely-marked gerbil may lack other good features. For this reason, it is prudent to restrict breeding to only one or two varieties so that you can maintain a good-

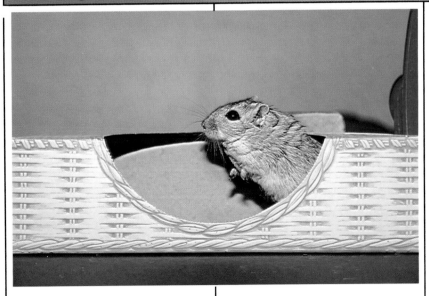

An empty tissue box makes for a convenient temporary "burrow." (Its occupant will likely shred it to bits with his teeth if he is left to his own devices.)

sized pool of stock with which to work.

7. Finally, the priority that should always head your list is that of good health. No other consideration is more important. There is no merit in producing stock with excellence in one or two features if most of that stock has a record of being very prone to illness. It is not a case that the virtues in your stock are linked in any way to the illnesses but simply that your original stock may have been weak in terms of resistance to pathogens.

If you have been conducting any form of inbreeding (which includes linebreeding), this will tend to fix in health weaknesses in the same way that it will have done with the virtues. When this happens, there is little alternative but to introduce an unrelated quality gerbil to your stock (an outcross). However, it should have a proven record of being from vigorous stock. Via such an outcross you may be able to revitalize the health of future generations while rebuilding any lost qualities resulting from the use of this gerbil.

If you take up serious gerbil breeding and undertake it in a planned manner, you will find it a source of continual pleasure as well as one of excitement. As each litter matures, there will be the thrill of anticipating whether you have bred that super individual of your dreams. There will also be plenty of disappointments, but they will only serve to make the successes all the more enjoyable.

Gerbil Colors

The number of colors seen in gerbils hardly rivals those seen in mice, rats, rabbits, guinea pigs, and hamsters. However, there are enough to provide an interesting selection to the average pet owner as well as to give the interested color breeder sufficient choices with which to work and offer him a challenge. There is no doubt whatsoever that in the immediate future there will be additional colors, as well as coat types, from which to choose.

The gerbil has reached that stage in which much experimental breeding is taking place in order to develop new colors. By carefully recombining existing mutations and then crossing them with other mutations, the color range can be extended.

THE WILD-COLOR PATTERN

The wild gerbil varies in its overall color pattern depending on the area in which it lives. However, all color patterns of the wild gerbil are variations on a similar theme. The Mongolian gerbil is an agouti with a white- or light-colored belly. The fur is banded with yellow, brown, and black, the last color being at the tip of the hair. The famous ticked effect of the agouti pattern (named for the South American rodent of that name) is created by the combination of these colors.

The underbelly fur is much lighter and ranges from an off-white, to cream, to almost yellow at times. The yellow color is actually caused by secretions from the sebaceous glands in the skin of the belly. This

Agouti gerbil. Some gerbil owners like to simulate the environment of wild gerbils for their pet.

liquid is used as a form of territory marking. When you hear gerbils being described as normals, it is the wild-type color pattern that is being referred to.

as possible.

This color, more than any other, is affected by direct sunlight, which will tend to bleach it so that it appears brassy in places.

A black gerbil. The average pet-quality specimen of this color variety usually has some white hairs or even some small white patches. (Note the white on the claw.)

BLACK

The black gerbil was first discovered in the USA at an aerospace research center in Texas in 1978. Examples were sent to Europe, from which stocks have been developed. The average pet-quality gerbil will not be jet black all over because some white hairs, or even small patches of white, may invariably be present. The exhibition specimen should be as free of any other color

BLUE

The so-called blue gerbil is not what you might expect. It is really a gray of various degrees of darkness. However, it will no doubt get better with breeder refinement in the coming years. There is also the possibility that a dilution mutation may arise that will help in refining the color from black.

An agouti male and an argente female. They are being introduced for the first time.

ARGENTE

In a good specimen, the argente is a very impressive looking gerbil. Black tips on the hairs are not present, so the whole appearance is of a lighter color. This variety has also been called cinnamon, or golden. The removal of black pigment makes the underbelly color lighter and also affects the eye color, which becomes pink-red.

GRAY, OR CHINCHILLA

In this variety, the yellow pigment is removed from the hair to create contrasting black-brown and white hairs. They impart a gray, chinchilla, or silver appearance. The mutation has appeared more than once, the current form having been developed from laboratory stock—a quite common happening in rodents. If the brown pigment can be removed by selective breeding or by the appearance of another mutation, a very beautiful silver should be the result.

LILAC AND DOVE

These two colors are, in fact, rather similar, the dove being a lighter shade of the lilac. The latter color was produced by matings using black and argente stock. This resulted in a pink-eyed lilac gray. When these pink-eyed lilac grays were bred with pink-eyed whites, the dove was eventually produced. As with all colors, the shade can be lighter or darker depending on breeder selection in a breeding program for doves.

HIMALAYAN, OR PINK-EYED WHITE

The latter of the two names is probably the more commonly used because in gerbils a really good Himalayan pattern is not as yet seen. A Himalayan should have dark pigment on the nose, ears, feet, and tail, but in gerbils only the tail may have dark pigment. Some breeders are trying to establish a true Himalayan—others are working to remove the black in the tail in order to produce an albino look-alike.

As in the Himalayan pattern in any species, the dark pigment is not evident when the gerbil is newborn because it is thermo-sensitive. The pigment forms only at the bodily extremities because they are at a somewhat lower temperature than is the rest of the body. When a baby gerbil is born, the nest's temperature is too high for pigment formation. The Himalayan pattern thus begins to show itself after a few weeks, when the gerbil is spending more time in the outside world— as opposed to its nest.

CREAM

The cream gerbil is not really a true cream as is seen in other pets but is a look-alike produced by pairing pink-eyed whites to argentes. The pink-eyed dilution has the effect of reducing the pigment strength in the brown of the argente, making it a lighter color.

Ten-day-old youngsters. One is argente (also known as cinnamon, or golden) and two are doves.

ALBINO

An albino is an individual lacking any pigment whatsoever. Its eyes are red, which indicates the hemoglobin of the blood. The albino gerbil could easily be confused by a novice with the pink-eyed white, as they do look very similar.

WHITE-SPOTTED, OR PARTICOLOR

In this variety there is a variable amount of white seen in the fur. It is quite random in where and how extensive it is. Any color form can carry this mutation. It is equivalent to pied in birds, or piebald, magpie, or bicolor in other pets. The famous Dutch rabbit pattern is created by a similar gene that is called white spotting. It is hoped that a similar pattern may eventually be created in the gerbil, as it has in guinea pigs and mice. Sometimes, there may be no white in the fur, but there may be some inconspicuous area of white, such as on the underside of the foot pads or in the pits of the legs. Mating well-spotted gerbils to similar individuals would seem to be the only way in which the extent of the white can be increased, though it is also possible for two poorly marked examples to produce well-spotted offspring.

FUTURE COLORS

What colors and patterns can you expect to see in gerbils in the not-to-distant future? Based on those seen in the other most popular pets, the following are very strong possibilities.

Chocolate and other shades of brown. Presently, the gerbil is the only major pet in which a mutation at the black pigment locus has not yet appeared. It will considerably increase the potential range of colors as it is recombined with existing and new mutations.

Red. This may be created by one or two possible mutations. The mutation known as *extension* is the most sought after as it offers many potential expressions from yellow through to black. The black tipping is removed while the red pigment is intensified by breeder selection for what are called rufous genes.

Dilute. Again, only in the gerbil and hamster are there no dilution genes that act on the density of pigment locus. Dilution will enable a blue to be created; and in combination with the brown mutation just mentioned it will widen the range of that color also. If a Himalayan is developed, it will increase the color range within that pattern, as it will in all other patterns.

Black-Eyed White. This addition to the whites will be welcomed. Unlike most other color mutations, it is likely that it will be dominant in its mode of transmission.

Dappled and Roan Patterns. These patterns are always very attractive and can be seen in most colors. However, they are usually accompanied by problems if in the homozygous state, which simply means that they need to be bred to normal self colors in order to prevent such problems. This means that the expectations of obtaining them are reduced 50% in any litter. Further, establishing a good pattern proves to be very difficult.

Dutch. I am sure that the Dutch gerbil is a realistic possibility. Unlike roans, the pattern has no associated problems—other than establishing it. As in rabbits or guinea pigs, obtaining good exhibition-quality stock will be very difficult due to the random nature of the white spotting genes that create it.

Banded. This is a variation on the bicolor theme, though it is created by its own mutation. You can see this coloration in the hamster, in which it is very popular.

Tortoiseshell. The probability of seeing a tortie gerbil is much slimmer than for the other colors and patterns seen. It is the result of what is called a sex-linked gene.

Coat Types. It is almost a certainty that both long- and rex-coated gerbils will appear in the not-to-distant future. A satin coat may well also appear. The future for the gerbil is thus very bright, and there are great expectations of things to come within the fancy.

The gerbil's eyes are set fairly high up on a wide head, giving him a good field of vision.

Using Genetics in Breeding

The science of genetics has had a profound impact on the lives of all humans, whether it be through medical research into disease, in the growing of new high-yield grain crops, or in relation to increased dairy production or heavier weight in cattle. However, it is also playing a significant role in the development of pet varieties. The modern small-animal breeder has much to gain from an understanding of the basics of the subject.

An argente white spot and an agouti.

For most breeders of gerbils, genetics will have the most direct application in respect to color production, but its value in improving the general health of a given line of stock, as well as its overall quality, is equally important. However, while you can produce relatively rapid results in terms of using genetics in color breeding, the same is not so true of the other areas mentioned. This is because the factors that control them are not as easily manipulated as is color. Further, matters such as health and quality need much more careful monitoring, and they require that the breeder is able to make sound judgments in selecting breeding stock at each generation.

In this chapter, only the most fundamental aspects of the subject will be discussed because of the constraints of space. However, if you are able to master just the basic principles and concepts of the workings of genes, even this will put you at a decided advantage in your breeding endeavors. For one thing it should impress on you the importance of maintaining breeding records, and it will also highlight the crucial role of sound selection in relation to breeding stock.

While the subject will be explained largely via the genetics of color, never lose sight of the fact that genes control virtually all aspects of your gerbils, from their size to their ability to resist disease. Even parenthood and traits such as docility and aggression are subject to genetic influence. However, the last two traits just mentioned and most others are also greatly influenced by environmental conditions. The application of genetic knowledge has value only if all aspects of husbandry are attended to as they should be. Genes give your gerbils a very definite potential, but to what extent that potential is achieved will be determined by general husbandry.

WHAT ARE GENES?

All features of your gerbils are passed from one generation to the next via tiny cellular bodies called genes. They are arranged in a linear manner along strands called

The distinctive look of an agouti is created by the bands of color (yellow, brown, and black) on the hairs.

Agouti gerbils. Gerbils have long back feet, which enables them to balance in a standing position.

chromosomes. Within each body cell there are a number of pairs of these chromosomes, each containing probably thousands of genes. Genes act as units of coded information in telling the cell how it will develop. Each chromosome of a pair has the same number of genes on it and are so arranged that a gene controlling a given feature has a gene for that same feature at the same position on its opposite chromosome. The site of a given gene is called its locus (plural: loci). There is one exception to this identical paired situation: the sperm and the ova. In them, one of the chromosomes is longer than the other. They are the sex chromosomes, and they are designated as X (long) and Y (short). A male gerbil is XY, and a female is XX. They contain no color genes as far as is known in gerbils and are concerned only with matters of sexuality. A feature may be controlled by one pair of major genes, or it may be determined by many gene pairs. Most features are determined in this manner and are said to be under polygenic control. They are much more difficult to manipulate than are features controlled by major genes—such as color. Even color genes, however, are influenced by what are called gene modifiers. These modifiers have the power to intensify or dilute the shade of a color and can be selected for by a breeder in the same way that the major genes can.

HOW HEREDITY WORKS

The gene pairs mentioned are inherited one from each parent, so that if the parents both have an agouti color, the offspring will also have an agouti color. The offspring cannot inherit more genes from one parent than from the other, so neither sex is more important than the other in transmitting features. In reality, a male may prove to be more important for the simple reason that he has a greater opportunity to spread his genes in a population than does the female. While the female can physically give birth to a definite number of litters in a year, a male can sire many more litters—in theory almost an unlimited number for all practical purposes. This is the only reason that he may have greater value to a breeder of gerbils or any other form of livestock.

THE RANGE OF COLOR GENES

It is important to realize that when we say color is a simple aspect to understand in respect to how genetics works, this does not mean that there is only one pair of genes that control color. Color-controlling genes are numerous, though only a small number of them have been identified at this time in gerbils when compared to other pets such as dogs, cats,

rabbits, or mice. In understanding the genetics of color, you should think in terms of the effect of a number of gene pairs interacting to create the color that you see. For example, one pair of genes will determine whether or not any color pigments can be formed. Another pair will control the density of the pigment and another will control where that pigment is located in the fur or on the individual hairs themselves. Only by considering all of the known gene loci does the whole picture start to become apparent. Genes do not blend; they always retain their individuality. Apparent blending is the result of the ways that the genes interact with each other.

GENE DOMINANCE

A gene may act upon a feature in one of three basic ways. It may be dominant, incompletely

Gerbils sniff each other frequently, even when they are not mating.

dominant, or recessive. We need only consider the last two items at this level. When a gene is dominant, it will show itself visually when in single form. If it is recessive, both genes of a pair need to be for the same expression before it is effective. You will understand this better when we consider examples.

MUTATIONS

A mutation is a change within the chemical make-up of a gene. Once a gene has mutated, it thereafter expresses itself in a predictable manner. It is not fully understood why genes mutate, but such happenings are essential in creating new species. They also provide varieties of animals under domestic conditions. As the number of a species is increased in a population, there is an increased chance that mutations will appear. It is important that you fully understand mutations so we will look at an example.

The normal coat of the wild gerbil is called agouti, the individual hairs being banded in yellow, brown, and black to create the ticked pattern that is very common in many animal species. When a gerbil appeared that was black, something had obviously happened. Only when this happened could geneticists identify the mutational gene. In this instance, its effect was to cause the yellow-brown areas of the hair shaft to develop black pigment.

The mutation was named non-agouti, and the gene locus thus became the agouti locus. It was found that when an agouti gerbil was mated to one of these non-agouti (black) examples, all of the offspring were agouti. However, when some of these agouti offspring were paired to each other, some black gerbils appeared. When they in turn were paired together, all of the offspring were black. The non-agouti gene was thus an alternative form of expression to the agouti. A gerbil could thus inherit

A young black gerbil with prominent white markings. It may not be show material, but it can still make a very good pet.

either an agouti gene from each parent, a non-agouti from each parent, or an agouti from one parent and a non-agouti from the other.

Do remember that at any one locus there is a gene for that feature on each of the two chromosomes of a pair. The offspring will inherit one gene from each parent at a given locus.

GENETIC TERMINOLOGY

In order to make things easy to calculate when discussing a given feature, such as color, geneticists use a sort of shorthand to represent the genes. A dominant gene is represented by a capital letter while a recessive gene is indicated by using a lowercase letter. The two types of genes are given the same letter if they are for genes at the same locus. Thus, an agouti gerbil has the genotype of AA—each A representing a gene at the agouti locus. A black gerbil has the genotype of aa. This shows that it is the alternative gene to the A at that locus and is recessive to it. By using the same letter you do not overlook the fact that you are discussing the potential genes at the A or agouti locus, or at whatever locus is under consideration.

The actual appearance of a gerbil is called its phenotype while the way that appearance is created is called its genotype. An agouti gerbil has a single phenotype, but it may have two genotypes. They would be AA or Aa. The first one is described as being

These babies are 18 days old. They will be fully weaned in about a week or so.

homozygous, meaning it is purebreeding. The Aa is heterozygous, or non-purebreeding. The AA gerbil can only pass an A gene to its offspring, but the Aa individual can pass either an A or an a—never both. We will pair gerbils

They are described as being agouti split for non-agouti. This is written as agouti/non-agouti, that before the line being visual, that behind

The actual appearance of a gerbil is called its phenotype; the genetic makeup that gives a gerbil its appearance is called its genotype.

having these genotypes and calculate the theoretical results. If an AA gerbil is paired to another AA gerbil, then the offspring will inherit an A from each parent, so they too will be AA in genotype (agouti). If an AA gerbil is paired to an aa gerbil (non-agouti or black), the first parent will pass an A gene to the offspring while the aa parent will pass an a. All of the offspring will thus be Aa in genotype. As the A gene is dominant, and the a gene is recessive, the youngsters will appear agouti but will be carrying the a or non-agouti gene.

it being "hidden." We can show this as a formula as follows: AA x aa = Aa Aa Aa Aa.

THE RANDOM NATURE OF GENE FERTILIZATION

When working out the potential results of a given pairing, it is important to calculate every potential combination of the genes. This is because the genes unite in a random manner at fertilization and is why, in the formula just given, four offspring are shown. They are not actually offspring but combinations of the genes that can be produced from the given pairing and that may turn up in any given litter. It happens, in this instance, that each potential combination results in the same genotype of Aa. Either of the A genes of the one parent could combine with either of the a genes of the other, so there are four possibilities. In this instance, such a pairing can only yield agouti gerbils split for, or carrying, the non-agouti or black gene.

With this information about random combination we can now work out the full possibilities of permutations at the agouti locus. Always remember that they are theoretical expectations expressing the percentage of chances that they may turn up in a litter—which does not mean all of them will.

If you know the genotypes for the color of your gerbils, you can thus work out what your chances are of obtaining given colors without the need to actually conduct matings to find out. You can select the pairing that best suits your needs. This is why a potential breeder needs to purchase his stock from a breeder who can state what the genotypes of his animals are—or as far as is possible.

It should be mentioned that there is no visual difference between an agouti gerbil and one that is agouti but carrying the non-agouti gene. Only by test matings can this be determined, and it can be a time- and cost-consuming process. It is also of no importance which sex is which color in gerbils

---

POSSIBLE PERMUTATIONS AT THE AGOUTI LOCUS

AA x AA = AA AA AA AA — 100% agouti offspring

aa x aa = aa aa aa aa — 100% non-agouti black

AA x aa = Aa Aa Aa Aa — 100% agouti/non-agouti

Aa x Aa = AA Aa aA aa — 25% agouti (pure), 50% agouti/non-agouti, 25% non-agouti black (pure)

AA x Aa = AA Aa AA Aa — 50% agouti (pure), 50% agouti/non-agouti black

Aa x aa = Aa Aa aa aa — 50% agouti/non-agouti black, 50% non-agouti black (pure)

because, so far, all color mutations are inherited quite independent of the sex of the gerbil. In other species, certain colors, such as tortoiseshell, are related to the sex and are called sex-linked genes.

COMBINING TWO MUTANT GENES

The next aspect of color genetics that we can consider is what happens when two mutations are combined. For example, a recent mutation in gerbils is that for albino. This is a pure white gerbil with pink eyes. The eye color reflects the hemoglobin of the blood, not a color pigment, which is totally absent in a true albino. The mutant gene responsible for this "color" is found at the full-color locus, which is designated as C. A full-color gerbil is thus CC, while an albino is cc, the mutant gene being recessive. The potential combinations of gerbils showing full color or albinism are worked out exactly as they were for agouti and non-agouti.

We will pair a non-agouti black with an albino to see what we will obtain in the offspring. When combining two mutational forms, the most important thing you must remember to do is to show the full genotype of each of the parents. The black gerbil is, of course, aa at the A locus, but it is also CC, for full expression of color, at the C locus. The albino is cc at the full-color locus and is AA at the agouti locus (it may not actually be so, but this aspect will shortly be explained). The formula for the mating is thus: aaCC x AAcc = aACc.

The black gerbil can

A cinnamon gerbil. A basic knowledge of genetics will be very useful if you wish to breed for a particular color.

pass to its offspring only genes for a and C, while the albino can pass only genes for A and c. The genotype of all of the offspring must, therefore, be AaCc (I have transposed the aA to Aa, which is how it would normally be written: this in no way affects matters). The offspring will be agouti in appearance but split for both non-agouti (black) and for albino. In this instance, I have not shown all of the potential gene combinations simply because they will, of course, all result in the same genotypes.

Now, if you had no knowledge of genetics and had paired a black with an albino, you would no doubt be at a total loss to understand how you obtained only all normal agoutis from your black x albino parents. Most people would expect to get a few of each color from the mating—so again genetic knowledge is very useful to a breeder.

EPISTASIS

This term is used to describe a gene that has the effect of masking the presence of one or more

other genes at differing loci. The albino gene is a well-known example of this action. When in its double form, it overrides other genes in the gerbil's genotype. For example, it was stated that in our previous mating the albino was AA at the agouti locus, but it could equally have been Aa or aa. This is because the albino mutation prevents the formation of any pigment in the animal carrying the mutant gene in double dose (both genes of a pair at the full-color locus).

It is important to understand that the other color genes are still present but are unable to express themselves if there is no pigment. An albino can, therefore, be masking any color. When this fact is not indicated in a genotype, you must assume that it is masking normality at every other color locus.

An ivory female and a cinnamon white spot male sharing a snack.

OTHER GERBIL COLOR MUTATIONS

Apart from the mutations discussed, there are a few other loci that have been identified with mutations. One of them is the pink-eyed dilution, which is transmitted as a simple recessive designated as p. The effect of this is not only to change the eye color to pink but also to lighten the color of the fur by suppressing the formation of black pigment. The result is the argente gerbil. If the p gene is combined with the non-agouti black, the result will be the lilac, of the genotype aapp.

A gray, or chinchilla, mutation has appeared in which the yellow pigment is suppressed. If it is combined with the black, the result, ultimately, is a so-called blue gerbil. However, it is really a sort of gray. Blue is normally created when a dilution gene acts on black pigment to reduce its density.

There is a second mutation known at the full-color locus, and it is called the pink-eyed white. It is really a very mild form of the Himalayan pattern seen in other domestic rodent varieties as well as in rabbits and cats. In it there is some pigment formed on the gerbil's tail but not on the other bodily extremities. It is designated ch and is one stage higher than the albino at this locus. When more than one mutation is known to exist at a given locus, they are then arranged in a series based on their power of expression. Thus, full color is dominant to pink-eyed white (Himalayan) and it acts as dominant (more or less) to full albino.

Yet another mutation

that has appeared is the white spot or patched. It results in various-sized spots or blotches appearing in a very random manner in the coat. Unlike all of the other mutations cited, it is dominant in its action.

LETHAL GENES

A lethal gene is one that when present in double dose results in the prenatal death of the animal carrying it. Sometimes the animal may survive birth, but it invariably dies at an early age. When such a gene is known to exist, one must always pair an example of the mutation with a normal example, thus ensuring that the double-dose situation does not arise. This means that in all litters, half of the offspring will exhibit the mutation, and the other

A black female and a male Canadian white spot.

This pretty color variety is one of the newer ones in the gerbil fancy. It is a gray, or chinchilla.

genotype is not split for black but is masking it, so it would be written as ccaa. The black gerbil's color would normally be visible; but with no pigment as a result of the albino mutation, the animal cannot display this aspect of its genetic make-up. The non-agouti genes are still present, however, and will be transmitted to any offspring from that gerbil.

All that has been said in respect to color is applicable to other features of your stock. Unlike color, you cannot identify the virtues of a quality gerbil with formulas because these formulas can only be applied to mutations. If the gerbil was to have a long-coat mutation, which is quite probable in due course, you could identify it with a gene symbol, such as l, as you could with a rex coat, which would use an R or an r, according to the power of the gene.

If you find the subject of genetics interesting, you are advised to purchase college-level books on the subject as they will give you a really sound basic knowledge of the subject across a whole series of applications.

half will be quite normal and not carry it. You might wonder why anyone would wish to perpetuate such genes, but the mutation may be found attractive, e.g., taillessness in the Manx cat or crests in some normally non-crested birds. These lethal genes are mentioned in case such a mutation should arise in the gerbil as it has in other rodents.

COLOR BREEDING RECORDS

If you become a breeder, your records should always indicate, as far as is known, the genotype of your stock. If you have an agouti of unknown genotype, it should be shown as A-, the dash indicating that you are not sure if it is AA or Aa. Likewise, if you have an albino that you know is masking black, for example, this also should be indicated. Here, the

Exhibition

The exhibition side of the gerbil hobby is a fascinating aspect that will appeal especially to the breeder. It not only allows such people to have their stock evaluated by experts but also adds a touch of excitement to the gerbil fancy. It is the best means to determine if a given breeding program is developing as planned. The gerbil show is also very much a social-meeting place where enthusiasts come together and are able to exchange ideas. Many lifetime friendships are struck up at exhibitions. All gerbil hobbyists should try to visit a few shows before they actually purchase stock because shows are really the only opportunity of seeing the full range of colors at a single location.

SHOW VENUES

The exhibition side of the gerbil hobby is not organized on the scale that is seen in dogs or cats; it is a much more informal affair. This is one of its great advantages because it will not cost you a fortune to compete. Most shows are staged in small venues, which can range from village halls to community buildings, or special sections in county agricultural fairs. A show can be restricted to members of the organizing club, or it may be a show that is open to any owner. The open shows are normally much larger affairs. Gerbils are often exhibited in association with other small rodents, so a day at such a show is sure to prove interesting.

A judge and a youthful exhibitor pictured at a gerbil show in the U.K. Gerbil shows offer the opportunity for fanciers to see virtually all of the color varieties that are available and to meet and make friends with people who share the same interests.

A young agouti gerbil about to start his workout.

JUDGING GERBILS

The exhibition gerbil is judged against a standard of excellence that is prepared by a panel of experts of the national gerbil society of a given country. Various parts of the gerbil, such as the head, body, and tail, are allocated a number of points, as are the color and overall condition of the exhibit. Each gerbil is compared to this standard and accordingly placed in relation to others in the same class.

Class winners advance to compete against other class winners of the same color, and ultimately of other colors, in order to determine the best gerbil of either sex in the show. This is a very general overview of the system of judging; each country will have its own particular rules and procedures.

EXHIBITION CAGES

Gerbils, in common with hamsters, are exhibited in variations of the standard show cage designed for mice. This cage is known as the Maxey cage, named for its designer Walter Maxey, an early pioneer breeder of fancy mice. It is made of plywood and features a removable wire front. The exterior is painted black, while the interior is white or a light pastel color. The bottom is lined with a white-wood sawdust that will not stain the fur of the

exhibit as might the darker woods if they become wet due to urine or water that has been spilled.

Some exhibitors trans-port their gerbils in sep-arate cages and transfer them to the show cage at the venue. Others place the exhibit in the show cage and place one or more show cages in special carrying boxes. It is important that the show cage is maintained in spotless condition because marks can be deducted for poor presentation. The cage may not carry any marks of identification on it that might suggest who owns the exhibit. This gives everyone a fair chance. A numbered label is placed onto the cage so that the officials—as well as the owner—know which cages belong to whom. At the time of judging, the cages are taken to the judge's bench, where the exhibits are taken out and scrutinized by the judge.

Show cages can be purchased from specialty suppliers, or you can make you own by applying to your national gerbil club for a copy of the specifications.

THE EXHIBITION GERBIL

Although all gerbils look much the same to the average person, if you see a number of quality show specimens and then compare them with the average pet, you will immediately notice the differences. They will be in relation to the shape of the head, the size, the tail, the texture of the fur, and especially to the color. To produce good show specimens, a breeder must carefully upgrade his stock over many years. This

The tip of a gerbil's tail is delicate and should *never* be used to pick up the animal: the skin could tear, which will cause the animal much pain.

The gerbil's long rear kangaroo-like legs help him to evade predators in the wild.

necessitates very rigid selection for required features. At the same time it is essential that the gerbils are fed correctly and kept under the best of conditions.

It is also very important that a potential exhibition gerbil is handled frequently so that it is never nervous during handling. If it bites the judge, this will not do its chances any good at all! From an early age, the show gerbil should be placed into an exhibition cage so that it becomes a familiar environment to the gerbil. The idea is to duplicate as far as is possible the conditions that will be prevalent at the show.

It is against the rules to in any way attempt to alter the appearance of the exhibit. In particular this means that you cannot dye or otherwise try to improve the color, or mask unwanted patches of white, for example. You can bath the exhibit if this is felt necessary, though bathing is not normally needed with these very clean little animals. You can use a silk cloth or chamois leather to groom your gerbil. This will bring out that extra sheen to the coat.

MANAGING A SHOW TEAM

Each exhibitor develops his own way of selecting and managing a show team, but the following will give you a basic idea of how to go about it. In the spring and early summer you can review all of that year's offspring. They should be graded on a continuum against fixed standards that you have established. Assess the stock that you plan to retain and compare them as would a judge. From the retained stock you can pick out your show team. It is recommended that the show stock be housed quite apart from the rest of the stock.

The reason for this is that the show gerbils will, of course, be traveling to and from many venues—all of which represent a potential means by which they may contract unwanted bacteria. At a show there are many other gerbils, some of which may, unbeknown to their owner, be incubating an illness. In the unfortunate case that your stock should become afflicted with a problem, it is better that it is restricted to the show stock rather than exposing all the other gerbils that you own to the problem.

Many exhibitors do not always regard isolation and special treatment of show stock as being as important as do other exhibitors. Only when they are faced with an outbreak of a disease do they then have reasons to regret their lax management methods. Years of hard work and endeavor can easily be wiped out by negating the importance of such husbandry.

Gerbils do not seem to suffer unduly as a result of being exhibited. Nonetheless, do not assume that they do not become stressed to a greater or lesser degree as a result of transportation and changes to their environment, which showing obviously entails. With this in mind, it is best not to risk overtaxing the energy of your show stock by exhibiting them too often. Give them a break between shows in which to rebuild their full physical vigor. This means that you

It doesn't take much to please a gerbil. Even an ordinary flowerpot can be used for his amusement.

should have a team of the size appropriate to the number of exhibitions in which you wish to participate.

Never exhibit a gerbil that you are not totally satisfied is in the peak of condition. Again, if the team is large enough in numbers, you will never be tempted to take a gerbil to a show simply because it is one of only a few that you have. Should you have a need to bath one or more of your exhibits, this should be done about seven days prior to the show so that the natural skin oils are able to give the fur its usual sheen. As the show day gets closer, do not feed your exhibits any food items such as beets, which might stain the fur—especially that of light-colored varieties.

When traveling to and from a show, always ensure that your stock is kept warm and away from drafts. A simple chill can develop very rapidly in such small animals. It could ruin the chances of a given individual getting an award if it should look a little "off color" when the judge examines it. Always allow plenty of time to get to the show venue early so that you are able to give your gerbils a final polish and give them time to settle

down to the environment before they are judged.

If after returning from a show you feel that one of your exhibits does not look its usual perky self, do not place it back with the show stock. Instead, immediately place it into heated isolation quarters where it can be observed for a day or so. Why take chances when you do not need to?

ENTERING A SHOW

To enter a gerbil exhibition, you must first write to the organizing secretary of the club sponsoring the show and request an entry form. With the entry form you will receive a copy of the rules and regulations as well as a show schedule of classes. There is a deadline date for entries so it is important that you complete the entry form as early as possible. Be sure to enter each of your gerbils in the correct class according to their sex, color, and previous status—meaning the classes restricted to novices that have not previously won awards.

If in doubt, contact the secretary or a gerbil exhibitor who can advise you as to which classes to enter. The completed form should be returned to the secretary along with the appropriate fees. You will

receive a show pass and labels for your show cages. Keep a copy of your entry form with you when you go to the show. In the event that an error has been made and you are scheduled for a class that you did not enter, you can discuss this with the show secretary and hopefully have the matter corrected. If you entered the wrong class, your fee will be forfeited and that particular gerbil disqualified.

PLAN THE SHOW SEASON

Although exhibiting is great fun, it can be both a time- and cost-consuming area of the hobby. The show season is normally during the autumn and winter months, when breeding activities are over or at a low level for many people. Plan your shows so there is ample time between them. While you are away from the breeding room you cannot be attending to a number of the tasks that need doing on a regular basis. You will need someone to cover for you while you are away on the weekends.

Gerbils may be only small and relatively inexpensive pets, but nonetheless their show management and planning is every bit as important as if they were high-cost purebred horses or dogs. The potential prizes and rewards earned by winning gerbils is never such that you can cover your costs. However, you will find that once you get into the swing of exhibitions, they will be a continual source of pleasure that you will look forward to—even if you are not a regular winner.

This male gerbil is very protective of his female partner, who is asleep.

Gerbil Health Care

One of the problems incumbent with any small pet, be it a gerbil, a finch, or a fish, is that it is very difficult to successfully treat should it fall victim to any major disease. More often than not, the animal will die without having displayed any external signs of illness. This is because animals can mask problems very well and because their metabolism is so rapid that pathogens are able to act on them quickly. One of the benefits of having a rapid metabolism is that such animals can also recover from a problem in an equally fast time.

ROUTINE HYGIENE

Easily the best defense that you have against pathogens (disease-causing organisms such as bacteria, viruses, and fungi) is simple routine hygiene. Many problems that occur in breeders' establishments could have been avoided had general husbandry techniques been better. Unfortunately, it

Your gerbil should be checked regularly for parasites. If you do discover evidence of these bothersome pests, check with your pet shop, which carries products that are specially formulated for the treatment of parasites in small rodents such as gerbils.

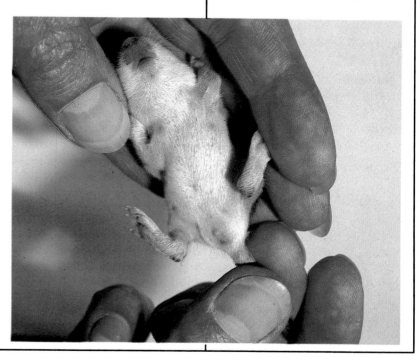

takes only one area of hygiene to be lax for pathogenic colonies to become established. Because the pet gerbil lives in a relatively isolated

accommodations.

After removing the floor material examine the state of the floor itself. Rust can develop in metal cages. When rust is seen, you

All of your gerbil's accessories should be cleaned on a regular basis to keep them germ free.

environment it is far less at risk to illness than is stock being accommodated in large numbers. Even so, each of the following aspects to be discussed is applicable to the pet owner. Let us review the more obvious ways in which bacteria may establish themselves in your cage(s).

1. Floor and Bedding Material. If either of these materials is allowed to become excessively dirty, it will not only provide an ideal site for pathogens and parasitic organisms such as lice or fleas but will also encourage flies to lay their eggs in the material. Clean all cages at least once a week and more often if a number of gerbils are housed in the

should use sandpaper or similar abrasive paper to clean the area; and then repaint it. Always clean the metal bars of the cages.

2. Food and Water Containers. These items can become a source of problems if they become dirty. They should be cleaned daily. Dispose of any that become cracked or chipped—and always keep spares on hand. Breeders should number each vessel (thus each cage) so that it is returned to the same cage from which it came.

3. Food. Never feed any item that you are not satisfied is really fresh. Store dry food in a clean dry area. Remove all soft foods (fruits, vegetables, and mashes) that remain

A healthy gerbil will respond with eagerness when it is offered its favorite treat.

uneaten after a few hours. Inspect the bedding area for any food that your pets have stored away but not eaten.

4. If you have gerbils in two or more cages, always wash your hands after handling the pets in each cage. Whenever you handle ill gerbils this is even more important. You can purchase inexpensive disposable surgical gloves: wearing them is recommended when ailing pets are handled. If you have many gerbils in a breeding room, wearing a nylon overall is also a good safeguard against pathogens and parasites alighting on your clothes.

5. Breeders should always ensure that no piles of rotting vegetation are situated near their breeding room. Such material is an obvious source of all kinds of pathogens, especially those of which happen to be extremely difficult to eradicate once they colonize your accommodations. Ringworm, a very undesirable skin condition, is caused by a fungi, not a worm.

6. Breeders should be really sure that their gerbil room is mouseproof and ratproof. These other rodents will delight in eating your pets' food and are obvious carriers of many diseases (most of which I should add are not carried by domestic mice and rats).

QUARANTINE

If you are satisfied with the general hygiene that you maintain, then the next source of potential pathogenic introduction will come when you add other gerbils to your stock. The only way that you can minimize the danger that this situation could present is by quarantining all extra gerbils that you purchase. The isolation period should be 14-21 days. It should safeguard you against most known diseases, which should manifest themselves over this period.

While stock is in isolation you can routinely treat it for external parasites (e.g., lice) with any of the proprietary treatments available from your pet store. Such treatments will kill all parasitic arthropods though you will also need to repeat the treatment some days later in order to kill larvae as they hatch from eggs. (The eggs are usually not affected by the treatment.) The quarantine period also gives you the opportunity to study the feeding habits of the new arrivals, more so than might ordinarily be the case once they are in the main breeding room.

A final comment in respect to bacteria being introduced to your stock is in relation to pathogens that may be carried into the breeding room by yourself or others. If you are a diligent breeder, you will be aware of your own hygiene standards, so your concern should be in respect to others. The hard reality is that not every breeder maintains high standards. Should such a breeder have an outbreak of disease in his stock and then visit you for one reason or another, there is the possibility that he will introduce the problem, via his clothes, to your stud.

Some breeders are very aware of this, and are extremely cautious as to whom they let into their breeding rooms—especially if they know that the visiting breeder seems to have a lot of illness problems with his stock.

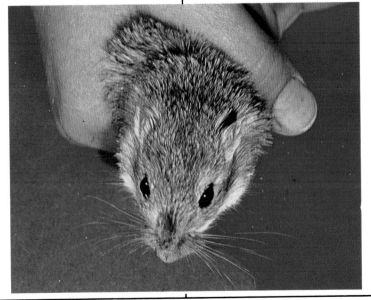

This unfortunate gerbil has a bare spot on its nose, resulting from its rubbing its nose against the bars of its cage.

An agouti gerbil investigating his wood block.

Such situations can be delicate—but it's your stock that is at risk, so you must ponder your own policy.

DIAGNOSING AN ILLNESS

Having taken every reasonable precaution to protect your stock, there is still no guarantee that an illness will not arrive by some means or other. Pathogens are always present in the air, and stressed stock may fall victim to them. Illness may arrive via food, for example, in spite of precautions, so it then becomes a case of identifying the problem and taking prompt action to arrest and overcome the situation.

As stated earlier, you may not see any clinical signs of an illness, but any change in the behavior or eating patterns of a gerbil should be regarded with concern. If it is not the only sign of an impending illness, it will usually be the first. A gerbil can have an off day just as you or I can, but this should correct itself within 24 hours. If it does not, you should assume the worst; and isolate the pet immediately. The same course of action should likewise be taken if any of the following signs are seen:

1. Diarrhea. This may be due to an excess of greenfood, a chill, or a

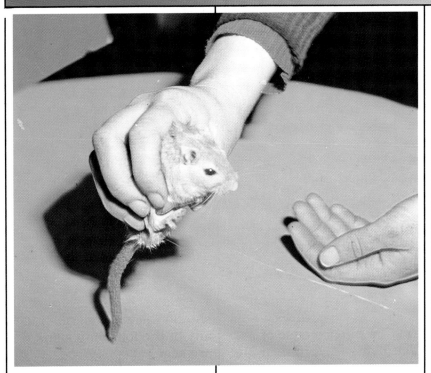

This is the wrong way to hold a gerbil: *never* squeeze the animal.

simple tummy upset—but it may indicate a more serious problem.

2. Bloodstreaked fecal matter. This is a more serious problem.

3. Bald patches in the fur, especially if the skin appears dry and flaked or has sores of a whorl-like nature. This may be a fungal infection (ringworm), or it may be due to a burrowing skin parasite.

4. Excessive scratching. All animals scratch themselves periodically but should not do so on a very regular basis. This usually indicates a parasite such as lice or fleas. In turn, these pests usually indicate unclean living conditions.

5. Any indication of difficulty in breathing—such as wheezing noises. This could possibly be a respiratory disease resulting from dampness caused by excess urine. There are many other possible causes.

6. Epileptic-type seizures. Invariably of genetic origin and not uncommon in gerbils.

7. Cuts and abrasions. Usually the result of fighting or because there is some sharp object (e.g., cage bars) that has pierced the gerbil's skin.

8. Any other signs of a problem, such as saliva around the mouth, which may be due to misalignment of the incisor teeth.

TREATING THE ILL GERBIL

Having reached the stage where the ill gerbil has been identified and isolated, the next thing that must be done is to try and overcome the problem in one way or another. This, of course, assumes that you actually know what the problem is. Some of the realizes that a given condition is not one that he can diagnose and he does not seek veterinary advice, he is rather foolish.

While the vet's fee may be greater than the ill gerbil's value, it begs the question "Is it greater than the entire stock owned by the breeder?" All of the

conditions mentioned may respond to home treatment, but others will not and may need microscopy of blood or fecal matter to determine the illness, its treatment, and cause. The reality is that with such low-cost pets, most breeders, and indeed many pet owners, will not take the gerbil to the vet because the fee will exceed the value of the pet. If this is so and the illness is serious, then being quite honest, the gerbil will die sooner or later. If a breeder stock is at risk if the problem is not identified and the cause established. The vet may not be able to save the ill gerbil, but by identifying the problem a course of action might be possible that will stop the illness from spreading; and the ill pet just might be saved by antibiotics or other modern treatments. Simple basic ethics would suggest that either the gerbil should be treated or the vet be asked to painlessly destroy it if nothing can be done. I will add—though you should not count on it—that some vets are sympathetic to the dilemma of costs that can be incurred by gerbils and other small pets invariably owned by children. As a good-will gesture, they may offer special low-cost fees for treating such pets. You will never know this if you do not visit them.

There are home treatments for some problems. A hospital cage should be part of your equipment if you are a breeder. A chill or minor digestive upset may correct itself if you withhold greenfood for at least 36 hours. Some form of heat

consulted.

Minor cuts should be bathed and treated with a suitable antiseptic, and the injured gerbil should be kept in isolation until the wound has healed. Doing so will overcome the risk of secondary infection, should it occur, being transmitted to other gerbils.

Skin parasites should be treated with proprietary remedies, and the infested gerbils should be kept in isolation until the repeat treatment has had time to totally eradicate any parasites on the skin. At the same time, all cages should be thoroughly cleaned, bedding and floor coverings discarded, and all

Depending on how much your gerbil gnaws, wooden toys may have to be periodically discarded and replaced with new ones.

treatment may cure a minor chill that is not accompanied by diarrhea. If diarrhea persists beyond 48 hours and the gerbil shows no inclination to eat, the vet should be

feeding receptacles washed. Destroy any wooden objects in the cage, and be sure to clean all shelves and crevices as they are places where parasites can easily breed.

Ringworm is difficult to eradicate because the spores of this fungus have a high resistance to treatment. Usually, only high temperatures are the only sure way to kill the spores. Consult your vet for a treatment for the gerbils themselves.

Seizures can only be left to run their course. Keep the gerbil in a quiet spot and do not handle it. Let it recover by itself. Very often it will be quite all right until the next seizure. Do not breed such a gerbil as this condition is often hereditary.

Respiratory and other internal dis-orders can be treated only with modern drugs from your vet. All that you can do is to be very sure that the accommodations are really well cleaned. Also, overcrowding may be a cause of the problem, so reduce the numbers of your stock or expand the housing facility.

If the gerbil has slobbers, the term applied to dental problems, your vet can trim the teeth periodically. Do not breed such a gerbil. If the condition is not treated, the poor gerbil may well starve because it is unable to feed correctly. Even worse, its teeth may continue to grow; and they may actually pierce the jaw with which they come into contact.

THE HOSPITAL CAGE

The breeder can invest in a com-mercially made small-animal hospital cage. These commercial units vary in price according to their specifications. They are often advertised in the cage-bird magazines as bird breeders are the main purchasers of them at the

Diet is an important factor in your gerbil's overall good health and appearance.

pet level.

The hospital unit must be thoroughly cleaned, disinfected, and rinsed after each patient has used it. If the problem with a given gerbil is only of a

normal room temperature. The gerbil can then be returned to the breeding room.

The pet owner who does not have a special hospital cage can place his pet's

minor nature, it is highly probable that heat treatment alone will effect a recovery.

Once a patient appears to be responding to a given treatment, the treatment should be continued until completion as directed by the vet. If the treatment is discontinued prematurely, this may result in a relapse, which may be much more difficult to overcome. This is because the surviving pathogens may develop their own immunity to the treatment. After complete recovery, you should gradually reduce the hospital-unit temperature a few degrees per day until it is back to

cage in a warm room and ensure that there is plenty of hay or other bedding material in the nestbox. He can also suspend a small light bulb over the cage in order to raise the temperature to that which has been recommended by the vet. By adjusting the height of the bulb, the temperature can be controlled.

POSTMORTEM

In the event that one or more gerbils should die within a short period of time, it would be reasonable to suppose that the cause of death was not natural. A postmortem of the bodies is therefore

Three popular gerbil color varieties: a white, a black, and an argente.

recommended. Your vet can arrange this for you. In the event that you cannot get the body to the vet the same day that the gerbil(s) died, you should place it in an airtight container wrapped in cellophane, and store it overnight in the refrigerator—never in the freezer compartment.

A postmortem may not always reveal the cause of death because pathogens desert a dead host rather quickly. It is thus a case of seeing which, if any, internal organs display signs of damage and then theorizing on which are the pathogens likely to have caused death. This procedure may save the lives of many others of your stock.

Remember, your best defense against disease is by feeding your gerbils a balanced diet and by maintaining very high standards of hygiene. For breeders, ensuring that stock never becomes overcrowded is an additional safeguard. This does not mean just in terms of gerbils per cage but also in relation to the number of gerbils kept within a single building.